FREEZER MEALS

The Only Recipes for Simplifying Your Daily Routine

(Delicious Make Ahead Meals Recipes and Freezer Meal Recipes)

Margaret Sarris

Published by Alex Howard

© **Margaret Sarris**

All Rights Reserved

Freezer Meals: The Only Recipes for Simplifying Your Daily Routine (Delicious Make Ahead Meals Recipes and Freezer Meal Recipes)

ISBN 978-1-990169-54-0

All rights reserved. No part of this guide may be reproduced in any form without permission in writing from the publisher except in the case of brief quotations embodied in critical articles or reviews.

Legal & Disclaimer

The information contained in this book is not designed to replace or take the place of any form of medicine or professional medical advice. The information in this book has been provided for educational and entertainment purposes only.

The information contained in this book has been compiled from sources deemed reliable, and it is accurate to the best of the Author's knowledge; however, the Author cannot guarantee its accuracy and validity and cannot be held liable for any errors or omissions. Changes are periodically made to this book. You must consult your doctor or get professional medical advice before using any of the suggested remedies, techniques, or information in this book.

Table of contents

Part 1 1
Introduction 2
Chapter 1: Freezer Meals – An Overview 3
Breakfast 3
Berry-Blue-Berry Oatmeal Yogurt Pancakes 3
Easy Tofu Scramble Wraps 5
Simple Breakfast Quesadilla 7
Seriously Sweet Potato Waffles 9
Early Rise Raisin Breakfast Bars 12
Lunch 14
Zesty Butternut Squash & Black Bean Burger 14
Tasty Tofu Mexican Bowl 17
Overloaded Veggie Soup 19
Steamy Vegetable Chili 21
Sweet And Zingy Pizza 23
Dinner 24
Veggie Jambalaya 24
No-Meat Veggie Meatloaf 26
Peanut And Sweet Potato Stew 28
Black Bean And Spinach Enchilada Casserole 30
Apple Cider Glazed Tofu 33
Fresh Veggie Pizza 35
Flavorful Barbecued Tofu And Vegetables 36
Dessert 38
Vegan Pumpkin Cheesecake 38

Non-Dairy Raspberry Mango Mint Smoothie	40
Rich Coconut Kiwi Smoothie	42
Sugar-Sprinkled Pastry Puffs	43
Sweet Strawberry And Pistachio Cookies	45
Chapter 2: Recipes	53
Breakfasts	53
Nutty Banana Cookies	53
Oatmeal Brownies	55
Ham And Cheese Muffins	56
Chocolate Banana Waffles	58
Midday Meals	59
Honey Glazed Chicken	59
Roasted Golden Vegetable Soup	61
Corny Tuna Fritters	63
Pepper Stuffed Meatloaf	65
Evening Meals	66
Fish Pie	66
Chicken And Pumpkin Pot Roast	68
Saucy Meatballs	69
Bobotie	70
Part 2	72
Introduction	73
Why You Need The Crockpot Miracle In Your Home	74
Great Tips For Using Your Crockpot	77
Safety Tips When Freezing And Defrosting Food	79
Slow Cooker Chillis	83

- Paleo Jalapeno Chili 83
- Sweet Potato Chili.. 85
- Best Ever Crock Pot Chili 87
- Pork & Black Bean Chili 89
- Turkey Chili 91
- Easy Crockpot Chili.. 92
- Thai Red Curry With Kabocha Squash 93
- Slow Cooker Seafood & Fish 95
- Seafood Stew... 95
- Coconut Curry Shrimp.. 97
- Thai Seafood Boil 98
- Lemony Tilapia With Asparagus 100
- Citrus Tilapia 101
- Seafood Stew...102
- Shrimp Bisque..104
- Spaghetti Squash Shrimp Scampi 106
- Lime Cilantro Fish Tacos..107
- Greek Fish Stew 108
- Soups, Stews & Curries 110
- Fat Burner Veggie Soup 110
- French Onion Soup 112
- Detox Veggie Soup..113
- Hot & Sour Flat-Belly Soup..114
- Spicy Green Soup..115
- Red Onion & Apple Soup...116
- Chipotle Black Bean Soup 117

Irish Stew 118

Lemon Chicken Stew 120

Beef Chuck Cabbage Stew 122

Curried Chicken Stew 123

Oxtail Stew 125

Lamb & Cabbage Stew 126

Rosemary-Garlic Beef Stew 127

Beef Stew 129

Beef & Broccoli Stew 130

Chicken Curry 131

Chicken & Chickpea Curry 132

Madras Lamb Curry 134

Spinach & Lamb Curry 136

Chicken & Turkey 137

Thai Turkey Legs 137

Herbed Turkey Breast 139

Tangy Turkey Meatballs 140

Turkey Breast 141

Ginger Peach Chicken 142

Asian Chicken 143

Meat Recipes 144

Healthy Doner Kebabs 144

Short Ribs 145

Mocha Rubbed Pot Roast 146

Lamb-Bacon Chowder 147

Lemon Infused Lamb Stew 149

Beef Chuck & Green Cabbage Stew 151

Hearty Beef Stew 152

Curried Goat Stew 154

Tomato Bredie 156

Balsamic Pork 158

Vegetarian Recipes 160

Cinnamon Bread Casserole 160

Mushroom Stroganoff 162

Minestrone 164

Asian Saag Aloo 166

Three Bean Pilaf 168

Spicy Veggie Chili 170

Veggie Sloppy Joes 172

Spicy Lentil Stew 174

Lentil-Navy Bean Stew 176

Sweet Potato Veggie Chili 177

Ratatouille 179

Cauliflower 'Mashed Potatoes' 181

Chicken Recipes 183

Chicken Divan 183

Drunken Chicken 186

Chicken Fajitas 187

Baked Pasta 189

Part 1

Introduction

Discovering time to prepare an appropriate meal can sometimes become challenging however we've got you covered from breakfast time to dessert. Maybe you have children, a spouse, and to mention in addition to that work. Formulating a system so that you can be prepared ahead of time can make your life a lot easier. This can also release some valuable time for you to assist your children with their school work or an extra hour to get started in an exercise regimen. We have compiled delicious recipes for your household. These daily meals are freezer-friendly and simplistic. Food planning and cooking in advance is among the most effective ways to preserve time and money in the kitchen, while additionally enabling you to take pleasure in healthy and balanced made-from-scratch meals. It's also among the best methods to assist a friend or a loved one during a time of need. We have supplied you with a variety of delectable and healthy vegetarian meals in addition to nutritional facts that everyone will look forward to.

Chapter 1: Freezer Meals – An Overview

Breakfast

Berry-Blue-Berry Oatmeal Yogurt Pancakes

Prep Time: 10 minutes
Cook Time: 10 minutes
Total Time: 20 minutes
Yield: 4 servings
INGREDIENTS
1 2/3 cups all-purpose flour
2/3 cup old-fashioned rolled oats
2 tablespoons sugar
1 1/4 teaspoons baking powder
1/4 teaspoon baking soda
1/4 teaspoon salt
1 cup plain Greek yogurt
1 cup milk
4 tablespoons unsalted butter, melted
2 large eggs
1 cup blueberries
Maple syrup, for serving
INSTRUCTIONS
1. Preheat oven to 200 degrees Fahrenheit along with a nonstick griddle to 350 degrees Fahrenheit.

2. In a big bowl, blend flour, oats, sugar, baking powder, baking soda and salt.

3. In a big glass measuring cup or a second bowl, whisk together yogurt, milk, butter and eggs. Add mixture over dried ingredients and merge utilizing a rubber spatula just until moistened. Combine blueberries and carefully toss to intermix.

4. Slightly coat a griddle or nonstick skillet with nonstick spray. Scoop 1/3 cup batter for every pancake and cook until bubbles show up on top and bottom is nicely browned, about 2 minutes.

5. You can freeze whenever ready and serve with maple syrup.

Easy Tofu Scramble Wraps

Nutrition Facts
Serving Size 197 g

Amount Per Serving	
Calories 402	Calories from Fat 143
	% Daily Value*
Total Fat 15.9g	24%
Saturated Fat 8.9g	45%
Cholesterol 129mg	43%
Sodium 375mg	16%
Potassium 313mg	9%
Total Carbohydrates 54.9g	18%
Dietary Fiber 2.3g	9%
Sugars 12.7g	
Protein 10.9g	
Vitamin A 10% •	Vitamin C 10%
Calcium 16% •	Iron 20%
Nutrition Grade B+	

* Based on a 2000 calorie diet

Prep Time: 15 minutes
Cook Time: 15 minutes
Total Time: 30 minutes
Yield: 6 servings
Serving Size: 1 wrap

INGREDIENTS

14 oz. firm tofu, pressed for at least 30 minutes then crumbled
1 tbsp. nutritional yeast
1 tsp. turmeric
1 tsp. garlic powder
1 tbsp. olive oil
1 small onion, chopped
4 oz. shiitake mushrooms, stems removed & caps thinly sliced
3 c. torn kale, spinach, or chard leaves, tough stems removed (I prefer kale)

Salt + pepper to taste
6 medium whole wheat tortillas

INSTRUCTIONS

1. Merge tofu, natural yeast, turmeric, and garlic powder in a sizable bowl. Put aside.
2. Warm olive-oil in a large skillet over moderate heat. Combine onion; cook 5-6 minutes or until softened, stirring frequently. Insert mushrooms and cook 2 minutes more. Blend in greens and tofu.
3. Continue to cook, stirring frequently, until greens have wilted, 2-5 minutes.
4. Separate greens and tofu onto each tortilla and tuck like a burrito.
5. To freeze, wrap firmly in a sheet of plastic wrap and position wraps in freezer bag. To reheat, take away plastic and loosely wrap in paper towel. Microwave for approximately 1 minute on both sides. In the event that center remains to be cold, continue to microwave for 15 seconds at a time until heated up through.

Notes

You can utilize a tofu press to press your tofu, but if you do not have one, you can utilize this method.

Simple Breakfast Quesadilla

Nutrition Facts
Serving Size 120 g

Amount Per Serving	
Calories 93	Calories from Fat 48
	% Daily Value*
Total Fat 5.3g	8%
Saturated Fat 0.9g	5%
Trans Fat 0.0g	
Cholesterol 0mg	0%
Sodium 94mg	4%
Potassium 260mg	7%
Total Carbohydrates 6.8g	2%
Dietary Fiber 2.1g	8%
Sugars 1.9g	
Protein 7.0g	
Vitamin A 22% •	Vitamin C 11%
Calcium 15% •	Iron 11%

Nutrition Grade A
* Based on a 2000 calorie diet

Prep Time: 15 minutes
Cook Time: 15 minutes
Total Time: 30 minutes
Servings: 1
INGREDIENTS
1 large egg
3 egg whites
1/2 cup black beans, rinsed and drained
1/2 cup corn, rinsed and drained
1/4 red onion, minced
2 tbsp. chopped cilantro
3/4 cup reduced fat shredded cheese
1/2-1 tbsp. taco seasoning
3 low carb 8 inch tortillas (2 pts. each)
INSTRUCTIONS
1. Whisk the egg whites and egg jointly. Scramble in a skillet lined with cooking spray and put aside.

2. In a sizable bowl incorporate the black beans, corn, scrambled eggs, onion, cilantro, shredded cheese, and taco seasoning.

3. Place 1/3 of the mixture in each and every tortilla and fold over.

4. Put into the freezer on a dish or baking sheet padded with parchment for one hour. Take out and cover individually to store or place into a freezer protected bag.

5. To reheat, remove the quesadilla and microwave until cheese is melted. To reheat in a skillet, first microwave it to defrost and then heat in a skillet to get the outside nice and crispy.

Seriously Sweet Potato Waffles

Nutrition Facts
Serving Size 118 g

Amount Per Serving
Calories 176 — Calories from Fat 21
% Daily Value*
Total Fat 2.4g — 4%
Saturated Fat 0.7g — 3%
Cholesterol 62mg — 21%
Sodium 59mg — 2%
Potassium 632mg — 18%
Total Carbohydrates 26.4g — 9%
Dietary Fiber 5.7g — 23%
Sugars 2.2g
Protein 13.5g
Vitamin A 3% • Vitamin C 4%
Calcium 5% • Iron 15%
Nutrition Grade A
* Based on a 2000 calorie diet

Prep Time: 15 minutes
Cook Time: 10 minutes
Total Time: 25 minutes
Yield: 4 8-inch waffles
INGREDIENTS
1 ½ Pounds Sweet Potatoes
2 Cups flour (1 cup all-purpose, 1 cup whole wheat)
1 Tablespoon Baking Powder
½ Teaspoon Salt
6 egg whites (2 yolks reserved)
1 ¼ Cups Milk
¼ Cup brown sugar (firmly packed)
¼ Cup melted butter
1 Tablespoon grated orange zest
1 Teaspoon ground cinnamon
¼ Teaspoon ground cloves
1/8 Teaspoon freshly ground nutmeg
1 Teaspoon freshly grated ginger

INSTRUCTIONS

Place oven temperature to 400° F

1. Thoroughly clean the 1 1/2 lbs. sweet potatoes by immersing all of them in Luke warm water and then scrubbing them. Dry them, cover them in tinfoil and bake them at 400 degrees Fahrenheit. When completed, let cool... unwrap and scrape the potato meat from the skin into a sizable mixing bowl, composting the skin.

2. Mash the sweet potatoes until mostly smooth. They could be a little lumpy since it will simply add a bit of texture to the waffles.

3. In a different mixing bowl , mix 1 1/2 cup mashed sweet potato , 1 1/4 cup milk , 1/4 cup brown sugar , 1/4 cup melted butter , 2 egg yolks , 1 tablespoon of orange zest , and 1 teaspoon freshly grated ginger .

4. In a different mixing bowl , whisk all together the 1 cup all-purpose flour , 1 cup whole wheat flour , 1 tablespoon baking powder , 1/2 teaspoon of salt , 1 teaspoon ground cinnamon , 1/4 ground clove , and 1/8 teaspoon freshly grated nutmeg .

5. Blend the sweet potato mixture into the flour mixture and mix.

6. Then whip the egg whites. This works the best whenever the whites have reached room temperature. Whip them in a stand mixer (or hand mixer) until they form peaks.

7. In pieces, fold the egg whites into the sweet potato mixture.

8. Utilizing a warmed waffle iron, coat all of the sides with cooking spray then simply add a heaping cup of waffle mixture to the waffle iron. Generally based on the height and width of your iron. Cook them per your equipment's recommendations.

9. Freeze then simply unthaw them the evening prior to when you are planning to eat them. You may top them with crushed pecans and maple syrup.

Early Rise Raisin Breakfast Bars

Nutrition Facts
Serving Size 259 g

Amount Per Serving	
Calories 425	Calories from Fat 85
	% Daily Value*
Total Fat 9.4g	15%
Saturated Fat 5.6g	28%
Trans Fat 0.0g	
Cholesterol 25mg	8%
Sodium 321mg	13%
Potassium 1325mg	38%
Total Carbohydrates 74.1g	25%
Dietary Fiber 6.2g	25%
Sugars 9.1g	
Protein 11.5g	
Vitamin A 8%	Vitamin C 35%
Calcium 21%	Iron 16%

Nutrition Grade B+
* Based on a 2000 calorie diet

Prep Time: 10 minutes
Cook Time: 14 minutes
Total Time: 24 minutes
Yield: 8 Servings
INGREDIENTS
1 ½ cups cook and mash Lentils, Red
1 cup Almond Butter
½ cups Brown Sugar
1 tablespoon Baking Powder
1 tablespoon Vanilla Extract
1 tablespoon Coconut Flour
¼ cups Raisins, Golden
¼ cups chop Almonds
Freezer Containers
1 Gallon Freezer Bag
Supplies
Baking Sheets
Parchment Papers

INSTRUCTIONS

1. Blend lentils, almond butter, brown sugar, baking powder, and vanilla extract on minimal speed in a mixer.

2. Carefully fold in coconut flour, raisins and almonds. Lay circular Tablespoon size scoops onto a parchment paper lined cookie sheet.

3. Bake at 350F for 14 minutes.

4. Freeze when ready to serve enjoy at room temperature.

Lunch

Zesty Butternut Squash & Black Bean Burger

Nutrition Facts
Serving Size 48 g

Amount Per Serving	
Calories 253	Calories from Fat 159
	% Daily Value*
Total Fat 17.7g	27%
Saturated Fat 1.6g	8%
Cholesterol 0mg	0%
Sodium 5mg	0%
Potassium 475mg	14%
Total Carbohydrates 19.1g	6%
Dietary Fiber 1.4g	5%
Sugars 11.7g	
Protein 6.8g	
Vitamin A 0%	Vitamin C 1%
Calcium 18%	Iron 8%

Nutrition Grade C-
* Based on a 2000 calorie diet

Prep Time: 15 minutes
Cook Time: 55 minutes
Total Time: 1 hour, 10 minutes
Yield: 6 servings
INGREDIENTS
4 Cups butternut squash, peeled and cut into 1/2 squares (saving the seeds)
1 can (15 ounces) black beans, drained and rinsed
¼ Cup Quinoa
½ Cup Water
¼ Cup red onion, minced
3 cloves of garlic, minced
1 Serrano Pepper, minced
1 Tablespoon ancho Chili Powder
2 Tablespoons ground Cumin
¼ Teaspoon ground Coriander

¼ Cup Pistachios, finely chopped
1 Tablespoon Sea Salt
1 Cup Panko Bread Crumbs
½ Cup Cilantro, chopped
Olive Oil

INSTRUCTIONS

1. Toss 4 cups of butternut squash with sufficient olive-oil to cover and place it in a baking dish. In a pre-heated oven at 400 degrees Fahrenheit, cook the butternut squash for approximately 45 minutes or until it is really tender.

2. Scrub and thoroughly clean the butternut squash seeds then fry them in a small frying skillet over a medium-high temperature with 2 tablespoons of olive-oil. Once they just start to brown, move them to a paper towel padded colander and complete them with sea salt.

3. Draw 1/2 cup of water to a boil. Add 1/4 cup of quinoa, lowering it to a simmer and cover. Cook for approximately 10 minutes until the quinoa is tender.

4. Include the roasted butternut squash to a sizable mixing bowl and mash. Put in 1 can of black beans and mash these as well. Fold in the cooked quinoa, 1/2 cup of cilantro, 1 tablespoon of chili powder, 2 tablespoons of ground cumin, 1/4 teaspoon of coriander, butternut squash seeds, 1/4 cup of pistachios, and salt.

5. Lightly sweat 1/4 cup of red onion, 3 cloves of garlic and 1 serrano Chile in a small sauce pan with one tablespoon of olive-oil over a moderate heat. Fold that into the mixture.

6. Fold in 1 cup of bread crumbs.
7. utilizing a biscuit cutter, make up your veggie patties.
8. Include one tablespoon of olive-oil to a cast iron skillet and heat it over a medium-high temperature. Fry the burgers until browned on both sides, including more oil when needed.

To freeze, spread out uncooked patties on a parchment paper-covered baking sheet, cover up with plastic wrap, and then put in the freezer to firm up. After 60-90 minutes, remove the patties and store collectively in Ziploc bags.

Tasty Tofu Mexican Bowl

Nutrition Facts
Serving Size 157 g

Amount Per Serving
Calories 181 — Calories from Fat 39

% Daily Value*

Total Fat 4.3g — 7%
Saturated Fat 0.6g — 3%
Cholesterol 0mg — 0%
Sodium 1077mg — 45%
Potassium 517mg — 15%
Total Carbohydrates 31.8g — 11%
Dietary Fiber 4.1g — 17%
Sugars 3.9g
Protein 6.0g

Vitamin A 202% • Vitamin C 38%
Calcium 11% • Iron 19%

Nutrition Grade A
* Based on a 2000 calorie diet

Prep Time: 15 minutes
Cook Time: 45 minutes
Total Time: 1 hour
Yield: 4 SERVINGS
INGREDIENTS
5 cups Vegetable Broth/Stock
2 cups Brown Rice, Long-Grain
4 teaspoons Salt #1
1 cup chop Cilantro #1
4 tablespoons juice Lime Juice #1
8 teaspoons mince Garlic #1
½ cups Olive Oil
1 ¼ ounces Taco Seasoning
2 teaspoons mince Garlic #2
¼ teaspoons Salt #2
1 cup Water
2 ¼ cups dice Tofu, Firm
1 ½ cups Corn, Frozen

½ cups dice Onion
3 tablespoons juice Lime Juice #2
½ teaspoons Salt #3
¼ teaspoons Black Pepper
⅓ cups chop Cilantro #2
2 cups drain and rinse Black Beans, Canned
1 cup Mozzarella Cheese, Shredded (serving day)
2 cups chop Lettuce, Leaf (serving day)
4 tablespoons Greek Yogurt, Plain (serving day)

INSTRUCTIONS

1. Place vegetable broth and rice in a mid-size saucepan and bring to a boil. Decrease heat, cover, and then simmer for 20 minutes.
2. Take away from heat and allow to sit covered for a minimum of 10 more minutes.
3. Mix in salt, cilantro, lime juice, garlic, and olive-oil.
4. In a different bowl, whisk together taco seasoning, garlic, salt and water.
5. Add into a shallow dish and marinate with tofu for a minimum of 15 minutes.
6. Set tofu in a sauté pan over medium-high temperature.
7. Cook until warm. In a different bowl, merge frozen corn, onion, lime juice, salt, pepper, and cilantro.
8. Incorporate rice, tofu, and black beans. Top with corn salsa, cheese, lettuce, and Greek yogurt.

Serving Day Instructions

Rice, tofu and black beans may be dished up hot or cold. Top with salsa mix, cheese, lettuce, and Greek yogurt.

Overloaded Veggie Soup

Nutrition Facts
Serving Size 276 g

Amount Per Serving
Calories 706 — Calories from Fat 308

	% Daily Value*
Total Fat 34.2g	53%
Saturated Fat 7.8g	39%
Trans Fat 0.0g	
Cholesterol 18mg	6%
Sodium 218mg	9%
Potassium 416mg	12%
Total Carbohydrates 86.0g	29%
Dietary Fiber 4.6g	18%
Sugars 1.8g	
Protein 17.7g	
Vitamin A 5%	Vitamin C 5%
Calcium 25%	Iron 19%

Nutrition Grade B+
* Based on a 2000 calorie diet

Prep Time: 20 minutes
Cook Time: 2- hours
Total Time: 2-3 hours
Yield: 8 servings

INGREDIENTS

2 - 3 Tbsp. olive oil
4 large carrots, sliced
1/2 bunch of celery with leaves, chopped
2 medium sized onions, chopped
4 large cloves of garlic, minced
1 large green pepper
1 large red pepper
1 small head of broccoli, chopped
4 large vine ripened tomatoes, chopped
1 cup fresh mushrooms, sliced
1 (15 oz.) can Muir Glen Organic Fire Roasted Petite Diced Tomatoes
1 (15 oz.) can corn, drained

1 1/2 cups fresh or frozen peas
1 1/2 cups fresh or frozen fine green beans, cut into bite sized pieces
3 potatoes, scrubbed and diced with skin on
10 cups of water
3 Tbsp. tomato paste
3 large bay leaves
1/4 cup dried basil (I know that seems like a lot, but it adds so much wonderful flavor to the soup)
1 Tbsp. sea salt
1/2 tsp. black pepper
1/4 tsp. crushed red pepper flakes (optional)

INSTRUCTIONS

1. Layer your stock cooking pot with olive-oil and warm on moderate heat.
2. Begin with the carrots and sauté your vegetables.
3. Putting in one vegetable at a time until they may be all sautéed while stirring.
4. After all the vegetables are added in, slowly and gradually add the water, tomato paste, bay leaves, basil, salt, black pepper and crushed red pepper.
5. Combine, cover and turn heat to low-medium.
6. Let simmer on your oven top for 2 1/2 to 3 hours.
7. Switch off the heat.
8. Season with more with salt and pepper if you would like.

Freeze, cool to room temperature and store in plastic freezer friendly bags or a freezer friendly container. Serve up hot with fresh bread or rolls.

Steamy Vegetable Chili

Nutrition Facts
Serving Size 4460 g

Amount Per Serving	
Calories 1,472	Calories from Fat 301
	% Daily Value*
Total Fat 33.4g	61%
Saturated Fat 5.0g	25%
Trans Fat 0.0g	
Cholesterol 0mg	0%
Sodium 6165mg	257%
Potassium 6182mg	177%
Total Carbohydrates 275.2g	92%
Dietary Fiber 55.0g	220%
Sugars 63.9g	
Protein 44.1g	
Vitamin A 1204%	Vitamin C 907%
Calcium 34%	Iron 134%

Nutrition Grade A
* Based on a 2000 calorie diet

Prep Time: 10 minutes
Cook Time: 10 minutes
Total Time: 20 minutes
YIELD: Serves 6 to 8
INGREDIENTS

1 tablespoon sunflower oil
1 medium yellow onion, diced
1 cup shredded carrots
1-2 jalapeño peppers, stemmed, seeded, and minced
3 garlic cloves, minced
1/2 cup bulgur, rinsed
2 tablespoons chili powder
1 tablespoon ground cumin
2 cups diced fresh tomatoes (about 2 medium or 6 plum tomatoes)
1 1/2 cups tomato sauce
1 (15-ounce) can kidney beans, drained and rinsed
1 1/2 (15-ounce) cans black beans, drained and rinsed

1 1/2 teaspoons kosher salt, or to taste
Chopped fresh cilantro

INSTRUCTIONS

1. Warm the oil in a Dutch oven or sizable heavy cooking pot over medium-high temperature. Combine the onion, carrots, and jalapeño and sauté, stirring frequently, until the onion is soft and translucent, about 5 minutes. Put in the garlic and sauté for 1 minute. Add the bulgur, chili powder, and cumin and blend until nicely merged.

2. Mix in the tomatoes, tomato sauce, and beans. Bring to a boil, and then reduce the temperature, cover, and simmer, stirring occasionally, until the beans are tender, about 1 hour. Season with salt to flavor.

Freeze ingredients in an air tight container. Serve with a sprinkling of cilantro.

Sweet And Zingy Pizza

Nutrition Facts
Serving Size 248 g

Amount Per Serving
Calories 354 — Calories from Fat 37
% Daily Value¹
Total Fat 4.1g — 6%
Saturated Fat 0.5g — 3%
Trans Fat 0.0g
Cholesterol 0mg — 0%
Sodium 375mg — 16%
Potassium 1513mg — 43%
Total Carbohydrates 63.7g — 21%
Dietary Fiber 16.4g — 66%
Sugars 7.8g
Protein 19.7g
Vitamin A 91% • Vitamin C 34%
Calcium 11% • Iron 39%
Nutrition Grade A
¹ Based on a 2000 calorie diet

Prep time: 10 minutes
Bake time: 20 minutes
Total time: 30 minutes
Yield: 4-5 Servings
INGREDIENTS
1 frozen pizza (Use a rising-crust pizza)
1 cup fresh pineapple, diced
1/2 cup sliced red onions
1 jalapeño, thinly sliced (omit if you don't like spicy)
1/2 cup shredded mozzarella cheese
INSTRUCTIONS
1. Preheat the oven as instructed on the packet for the frozen pizza, and line a baking sheet with parchment paper.
2. Take out the pizza from the packaging, and place it on the baking sheet.

3. Arrange the pineapple, sliced up red onions and jalapeños on top of the pizza.
4. Spread the mozzarella cheese on top of the pizza, and bake for 20 minutes or until the cheese has melted and the crust is golden brown.
5. Remove from the oven, and slice into portions. Freeze in an air tight container or freezer bags.

Dinner

Veggie Jambalaya

Nutrition Facts
Serving Size 70 g

Amount Per Serving	
Calories 66	Calories from Fat 23
	% Daily Value*
Total Fat 2.8g	4%
Saturated Fat 1.5g	8%
Trans Fat 0.0g	
Cholesterol 8mg	3%
Sodium 86mg	4%
Potassium 66mg	2%
Total Carbohydrates 7.2g	2%
Dietary Fiber 0.9g	4%
Sugars 4.7g	
Protein 4.4g	
Vitamin A 2%	Vitamin C 35%
Calcium 11%	Iron 1%

Nutrition Grade B
* Based on a 2000 calorie diet

Prep Time: 25 minutes
Cook Time: 40 minutes
Total Time: 65 minutes
Yield: Serves 6-8
INGREDIENTS
1 Tbsp. oil
1 onion, chopped
1 green bell pepper, chopped

1/2 cup chopped celery
3 garlic cloves, minced
2 cups water
14 oz. can diced tomatoes, undrained
8 oz. can tomato sauce
1/2 tsp. dried Italian seasoning
1/4 tsp. crushed red pepper flakes
1/8 tsp. fennel seeds, crushed
1 cup uncooked long grain rice
15 oz. can butter beans, rinsed and drained
15 oz. can red beans, rinsed and drained

INSTRUCTIONS

1. in a sizable skillet, heat up oil over medium temperature. Sauté onion, green bell pepper, celery, and garlic in hot oil until tender, about 3-4 minutes, stirring repeatedly.
2. Combine water, tomatoes, tomato sauce, Italian seasoning, red pepper flakes, and fennel seed.
3. Bring to a boil and combine rice. Decrease heat to low, cover up and simmer for 20-25 minutes until rice is tender, stirring repeatedly. Include beans and cover. Simmer 5-10 minutes longer or until nicely warm, stirring frequently.
4. Freeze, cool casserole in fridge and ladle into plastic air tight containers. To reheat, set frozen jambalaya in saucepan and heat over minimal heat, separating and stirring frequently, until hot.

No-Meat Veggie Meatloaf

Nutrition Facts
Serving Size 265 g

Amount Per Serving	
Calories 174	Calories from Fat 25
	% Daily Value*
Total Fat 2.8g	4%
Trans Fat 0.0g	
Cholesterol 0mg	0%
Sodium 352mg	15%
Potassium 260mg	7%
Total Carbohydrates 33.8g	11%
Dietary Fiber 3.1g	12%
Sugars 5.7g	
Protein 3.9g	
Vitamin A 22%	Vitamin C 59%
Calcium 4%	Iron 12%

Nutrition Grade A-
* Based on a 2000 calorie diet

Prep Time: 35 minutes
Cook Time: 110 minutes
Total Time: 145 minutes
Yield: 6 servings

INGREDIENTS
1 cup dried lentils
1/4 cup wheat germ
1 cup whole wheat bread crumbs
1/2 cup cooked brown rice
1 onion, minced
3 cloves garlic, minced
3 eggs OR 3/4 cup egg substitute
1 tsp. dried oregano leaves
1 tsp. dried thyme leaves
1 Tbsp. soy sauce
1/4 cup ketchup
1 Tbsp. olive oil
1/2 tsp. Tabasco sauce

1/2 tsp. salt
1/8 tsp. white pepper
INSTRUCTIONS
1. Preheat oven to 350 degrees Fahrenheit.
2. Position lentils in a compact saucepan and cover with water. Simmer over minimum heat for 60 to 90 minutes, or until tender. Drain lentils, if needed, and then coarsely mash lentils. Blend with remaining ingredients.
3. Add mixture into a 9 x 5" loaf pan sprayed with nonstick cooking spray. Cover with foil and bake at 350 degrees Fahrenheit for 30-40 minutes. Take off foil and bake for an additional 10-15 minutes or until loaf is firm to the touch.

Cover up, label, and freeze. Allow meatloaf thaw in the refrigerator over-night, and then reheat at 350 degrees Fahrenheit for 20 minutes

Peanut And Sweet Potato Stew

Nutrition Facts
Serving Size 111 g

Amount Per Serving
Calories 262 Calories from Fat 53
% Daily Value*
Total Fat 5.9g — 9%
Saturated Fat 1.2g — 6%
Cholesterol 82mg — 27%
Sodium 493mg — 21%
Potassium 505mg — 14%
Total Carbohydrates 39.0g — 13%
Dietary Fiber 11.7g — 47%
Sugars 4.3g
Protein 14.3g

Vitamin A 5% • Vitamin C 9%
Calcium 5% • Iron 22%
Nutrition Grade A
* Based on a 2000 calorie diet

Prep time: 10 minutes
Cook time: 45 minutes
Total time: 55 minutes
Yield: 4 servings
INGREDIENTS
2 tablespoons olive oil
1 medium onion, very finely minced
3 cloves garlic, finely minced
1 tbsp fresh minced ginger
½ tsp crushed red chili pepper
1 – 14.5 oz. (400 g) can crushed or diced tomatoes
½ cup peanut butter (or almond or sunflower butter)
1 tsp dried coriander (optional)
2 cups vegetable broth (or water)
1 medium sweet potato (about 1 lb.), peeled and diced
1 can kidney or black beans, drained and rinsed
1 ½ cups frozen peas (or frozen/canned corn)

2 cups hearty leafy greens (spinach, arugula, kale, collard)
Salt and pepper
INSTRUCTIONS
1. Combine diced tomatoes together with their juice for just a few moments in the food processor or blender, simply to break them up.
2. Heat up the oil in a sizable pot or Dutch oven over moderate heat. Combine the onion and cook until soft but not brown, approximately 10 minutes.
3. Combine the garlic, ginger and chili and cook for about 5 minutes to soften.
4. Combine the tomatoes, stir to blend then include the peanut butter (and coriander, if using), stirring it in until smooth.
5. Blend in the broth add sweet potatoes. Cover up the pan and simmer until the sweet potatoes are tender but not falling apart, about 15 minutes.
6. Combine the black beans, peas/corn, and greens and cook until the beans and peas/corn are heated up throughout and the greens are wilted.
7. Freeze in an air tight container. When serving season with salt and pepper, and add more crushed chili flakes, according to your heat preference.

Black Bean And Spinach Enchilada Casserole

Nutrition Facts
Serving Size 310 g

Amount Per Serving
Calories 366 — Calories from Fat 219
% Daily Value*
Total Fat 24.3g — 37%
Saturated Fat 4.7g — 23%
Cholesterol 0mg — 0%
Sodium 587mg — 24%
Potassium 655mg — 19%
Total Carbohydrates 26.8g — 9%
Dietary Fiber 7.4g — 29%
Sugars 10.1g
Protein 15.0g

Vitamin A 33% • Vitamin C 37%
Calcium 4% • Iron 31%

Nutrition Grade B+
* Based on a 2000 calorie diet

Prep time: 10 minutes
Cook time: 45 minutes
Total time: 55 minutes
Yield: 8 servings
INGREDIENTS
For the sauce
3 cups low sodium vegetable broth
¼ cup tomato paste
¼ cup all-purpose flour (I used whole wheat flour)
2 Tbsp. cooking oil (I used coconut)
2 tsp. cumin
¼ tsp. garlic powder
¼ tsp. onion powder
¼ tsp. chili powder
Salt/pepper
For the enchiladas
15 oz. can black beans, rinsed and drained

1 ½ cups corn (I used frozen, thawed)
6 oz. fresh baby spinach
6 green onions, thinly sliced
1/3 cup cilantro, chopped
2 tsp. cumin
3 cups shredded 3 cheese blend (or pepper jack, etc.)
8 whole wheat or flour tortillas (I only needed 6, due to my change at the end)

INSTRUCTIONS

1. To create the sauce, heat up oil over moderate heat in a saucepan. Combine tomato paste, flour, cumin, garlic powder, onion powder, and chili powder. Cook 1 minute, whisking. Whisk in broth, bring to a boil. Decrease to simmer, and cook until somewhat thickened, approximately 8 minutes. Salt/pepper to liking, and put aside. Ensure that you taste the sauce after seasoning. I did add a little more salt.

2. Sauté the spinach in oil over moderate heat for 1-2 minutes until slightly wilted. In a sizable bowl, incorporate beans, 2 cups cheese, spinach, corn, green onions, cumin, and cilantro.

3. Preheat oven to 375. Slightly coat a 9x13 inch baking dish with oil or cooking spray, and add a little bit of the sauce to coat the bottom. So, here is where 4. Layer it similar to a lasagna. Lie down two tortillas and cover them with half the vegetable mix.

5. Lay down two more tortillas down and top with the left over vegetable mix. Then add two more tortillas on the top and poured the remainder of the enchilada

sauce over them. Lastly, top it with the remaining cheese. Bake for 45 minutes or till golden brown.

Freeze using a large plastic air tight container. Warm in oven at 300 degrees Fahrenheit and serve.

Apple Cider Glazed Tofu

Nutrition Facts
Serving Size 246 g

Amount Per Serving	
Calories 195	Calories from Fat 44
	% Daily Value*
Total Fat 4.9g	8%
Saturated Fat 0.7g	4%
Trans Fat 0.0g	
Cholesterol 0mg	0%
Sodium 383mg	16%
Potassium 571mg	16%
Total Carbohydrates 34.0g	11%
Dietary Fiber 6.0g	24%
Sugars 3.3g	
Protein 6.8g	
Vitamin A 46% •	Vitamin C 20%
Calcium 9% •	Iron 22%

Nutrition Grade A
* Based on a 2000 calorie diet

Prep time: 30 minutes
Cook time: 1 hour 15 minutes
Total time: 1 hour 45 minutes
Yield: 4 servings
INGREDIENTS
2 lb. firm or extra firm tofu
Marinade
1 tbsp. vegetable broth concentrate*
2 tbsp. Braggs liquid aminos
3 tbsp. nutritional yeast
1 tsp dry mustard
1/4 tsp black pepper
2 cups apple cider
Glaze
3 cups cider
1/2 cup of the marinade
1/4 cup white wine**
2 tbsp. apple butter

INSTRUCTIONS

1. Drain out the tofu and press it for 30 minutes. After that cut the tofu 1/2 inch thick portions. Position the tofu in a single layer in a shallow dish.

2. Whisk the marinade ingredients all together, and pour over the tofu.

3. Refrigerate the tofu at least 12 hours, or up to 3 days ahead of time.

4. To bake, move the tofu to a baking dish, maintaining it in a single layer, without the marinade. Set 1/2 cup of the marinade aside. Bake for 90 minutes at 325 degrees Fahrenheit, basting with the left over marinade every 20-30 minutes.

5. Put together the glaze by blending the set-aside 1/2 cup of marinade, the cider, wine, and apple butter in a skillet or sauce pan.

6. Simmer over moderate heat, until reduced to about 3/4 cup volume. Combine frequently, to avoid scorching.

7. To serve, organize the baked tofu onto a platter. Drizzle with the glaze.

Freeze in an airtight plastic container until ready to serve.

Fresh Veggie Pizza

Nutrition Facts
Serving Size 555 g

Amount Per Serving	
Calories 350	Calories from Fat 94
	% Daily Value*
Total Fat 10.5g	16%
Saturated Fat 2.1g	10%
Cholesterol 0mg	0%
Sodium 42mg	2%
Potassium 900mg	26%
Total Carbohydrates 47.5g	16%
Dietary Fiber 4.5g	18%
Sugars 38.2g	
Protein 22.5g	
Vitamin A 0% *	Vitamin C 6%
Calcium 49% *	Iron 36%

Nutrition Grade A
* Based on a 2000 calorie diet

Prep time: 15 minutes
Cook time: 15 minutes
Total time: 30 minutes
Yield: 4 Servings
INGREDIENTS
1 frozen pizza (I used a brick oven-style pizza)
1 tablespoon dried Italian seasoning
2-3 medium-size tomatoes, sliced
1/4 cup sliced black olives
1/2 red onion, sliced or diced
1 handful fresh basil, chopped
INSTRUCTIONS
1. Preheat the oven to 300 degrees Fahrenheit, and line a baking sheet with parchment paper.
2. Take out the pizza from the packaging, and place it on the baking sheet.
3. Sprinkle the pizza with the dried Italian seasoning.

4. Organize the tomatoes, olives and red onion on top of the pizza.
5. Generously top with the chopped basil, and bake for 15 minutes or until the pizza is golden brown.
6. Freeze in a plastic air tight container or freezer bags.

Flavorful Barbecued Tofu And Vegetables

Nutrition Facts
Serving Size 12 g

Amount Per Serving	
Calories 20	Calories from Fat 17
	% Daily Value*
Total Fat 1.9g	3%
Cholesterol 2mg	1%
Sodium 74mg	3%
Potassium 2mg	0%
Total Carbohydrates 0.9g	0%
Protein 0.1g	
Vitamin A 1%	Vitamin C 0%
Calcium 1%	Iron 2%

Nutrition Grade C-
* Based on a 2000 calorie diet

Prep time: 15 minutes
Cook time: 15 minutes
Total time: 30 minutes
Yield: 2 Servings
INGREDIENTS
1 package of extra firm tofu
1/2 white onion
1/2 cup gluten free teriyaki sauce --unless you aren't gluten free.
2 Tsp white wine vinegar
1 Tsp Worcestershire sauce
1 table spoon cinnamon
1/2 t fennel

1/2 t ginger
1/2 t cloves
1/2 t red pepper flakes

INSTRUCTIONS

1. Drain out and squeeze tofu to release any excess moisture. This can be done overnight, by placing the tofu in a colander and setting a small plate on the top for a bit of weight.
2. Slice tofu into 1-inch pieces, and pan fry in some olive-oil until it is golden brown on all sides.
3. Leave the portions alone to obtain a good crust on them before flipping. After the tofu is done getting crusty, dice up your onion and get started making your sauce.
4. Combine all the liquid and spices straight to your crockpot stoneware insert. Toss the tofu in the marinade blend to coat thoroughly. Cover up and cook on low for 6 hours.

Freeze in a plastic airtight container and serve with steamed white or brown rice.

Dessert

Vegan Pumpkin Cheesecake

Nutrition Facts
Serving Size 18 g

Amount Per Serving	
Calories 10	Calories from Fat 1
	% Daily Value*
Total Fat 0.1g	0%
Trans Fat 0.0g	
Cholesterol 0mg	0%
Sodium 15mg	1%
Potassium 33mg	1%
Total Carbohydrates 2.0g	1%
Sugars 0.9g	
Protein 0.2g	
Vitamin A 2%	Vitamin C 2%
Calcium 1%	Iron 1%

Nutrition Grade A
* Based on a 2000 calorie diet

Prep time: 30 minutes
Cook time: 15 minutes
Total time: 45 minutes
Yield: 6 Servings
INGREDIENTS
2 cups almonds
1 cup dates
2 cups raw cashews
2 cups fresh grated pumpkin
1/2 cup coconut oil
3 tbsp. lemon juice
1/2 cup agave
1 tsp vanilla
4 tsp cinnamon
1 tsp nutmeg
2 tsp ginger
INSTRUCTIONS

1. Immerse cashews in water for a minimum of 30 MINUTES, and then drain.
2. In a food processor, mix the almonds and dates until finely chopped. Combine a tablespoon of water if that helps to get things moving. Press the mixture into the bottom part of a spring-form pan.
3. Wash-out the food processor and combine all the other ingredients until mixed and creamy.
4. Add mixture into spring-form pan and smooth out the surface. Cover up with aluminum foil, and allow it placed in the freezer for a minimum of 4 hours. This is going to harden the coconut oil and set the cheesecake. After this point, move the cheesecake in the refrigerator for a minimum of one hour before serving. Whenever opening the spring-form pan, carefully insert a knife along the edge of the cheesecake, to ensure that it does not stick to the edge of the pan.
5. Serve with raw chocolate sauce (1 tbsp. raw cocoa powder + 1 tbsp. agave syrup + 1/2 tbsp. coconut oil)

Non-Dairy Raspberry Mango Mint Smoothie

Nutrition Facts
Serving Size 218 g

Amount Per Serving	
Calories 725	Calories from Fat 502
	% Daily Value*
Total Fat 55.8g	86%
Saturated Fat 21.4g	107%
Trans Fat 0.0g	
Cholesterol 0mg	0%
Sodium 14mg	1%
Potassium 880mg	25%
Total Carbohydrates 52.7g	18%
Dietary Fiber 11.1g	44%
Sugars 25.5g	
Protein 15.5g	
Vitamin A 254%	Vitamin C 12%
Calcium 16%	Iron 31%

Nutrition Grade C+
*Based on a 2000 calorie diet

Prep time: 15 minutes

Yield: 2 Servings

INGREDIENTS

2 cups fresh raspberries, rinsed

2 cups cold water

1 1/2 to 2 large mangos, peeled and diced (1 to 1 1/2 cups diced)

14-20 spearmint leaves, rinsed

1 lime, juiced

Pinch of sea salt

2-3 cups ice cubes

Natural sweetener (optional)

INSTRUCTIONS

1. Mix raspberries and water and purée until smooth. Pour through a fine mesh stainless steel strainer and dispose of the seeds.

2. Return the raspberry purée to the blender and add the mango, a little over half of the mint leaves, lime

juice, sea salt, and ice cubes. Blend until smooth. If preferred, incorporate optional sweetener and left over mint leaves to taste, mixing after each addition. Best enjoyed immediately!

Recipe Notes

3. To make fresh mint simple syrup, combine 1/2 cup of water with 1/2 cup of white sugar and bring to a boil on the oven top. Remove from the heat and stir 1/2 cup chopped fresh mint into the liquid. Cover and let steep until it cools to room temperature. Strain to eliminate the mint bits and keep refrigerated for approximately two weeks.

4. Frozen mangos can be substituted for fresh, as can raspberries. If utilizing frozen raspberries, easily mix all ingredients and blend together; no need to strain the seeds.

Store ingredients in an airtight freezer container or in ice cube trays until ready for use

Rich Coconut Kiwi Smoothie

Nutrition Facts
Serving Size 597 g

Amount Per Serving
Calories 64 — Calories from Fat 7

	% Daily Value*
Total Fat 0.8g	1%
Cholesterol 0mg	0%
Sodium 132mg	6%
Potassium 190mg	5%
Total Carbohydrates 14.7g	5%
Dietary Fiber 8.0g	32%
Sugars 5.4g	
Protein 1.5g	

Vitamin A 1% • Vitamin C 54%
Calcium 4% • Iron 5%

Nutrition Grade A
* Based on a 2000 calorie diet

Prep time: 15 minutes
Yield: 2 Servings
INGREDIENTS
2 kiwis, peeled and quartered
1/2 medium avocado
1 cup coconut water
2 tablespoons canned coconut milk
1 lemon, juiced (more to taste)
4 to 5 ice cubes
INSTUCTIONS
1. Combine all ingredients in a blender and blend on high until smooth and creamy, place ingredients in ice tray.
Store ingredients in an airtight freezer container or in ice cube trays until ready for use.

Sugar-Sprinkled Pastry Puffs

Nutrition Facts
Serving Size 283 g
Amount Per Serving
Calories 367   Calories from Fat 248
                              % Daily Value*
Total Fat 27.5g   42%
  Saturated Fat 10.5g   53%
  Trans Fat 0.0g
Cholesterol 0mg   0%
Sodium 15mg   1%
Potassium 1041mg   30%
Total Carbohydrates 32.6g   11%
  Dietary Fiber 11.9g   48%
  Sugars 15.2g
Protein 4.3g
Vitamin A 6%   •   Vitamin C 253%
Calcium 7%   •   Iron 9%
Nutrition Grade B
* Based on a 2000 calorie diet

Prep time: 15 minutes
Cook time: 30 minutes
Total time: 45 minutes
Yield: 36 puffs

INGREDIENTS

1 1/2 cups water
1 plus 1 tablespoon unsalted butter, cut into cubes
1 teaspoon sugar
1/2 teaspoon salt
200 (about 1 1/2 cups) all-purpose flour
8 (large) eggs
Pearl sugar, for decorating (See Note)

INSTRUCTIONS

1. Preheat the oven to 400 Fahrenheit. Line 2 large baking sheets with parchment paper.

2. In a sizable saucepan, mix the water, butter, sugar and salt and bring to a boil. Decrease the heat to moderate. Insert the flour all at once and stir

vigorously with a wooden spoon until a tight dough forms and pulls off of the side of the pan, 2 minutes. Remove the pan from the heat.

3. In a bowl, whip 7 eggs and include in the dough in four batches, stirring vigorously between additions until the eggs are entirely combined and the pastry is smooth. The dough should be glossy and fairly slowly hang, stretch out and fall from the spoon in thick ribbons. If necessary, whip in the remaining egg.

4. Move the dough to a piping bag equipped with a 1/2-inch plain tip. Pipe 1 1/2-inch mounds onto the baking sheets, leaving 1 inch between them. Generously sprinkle each and every mound with 1/2 teaspoon of pearl sugar. Bake the coquettes for approximately 30 minutes, until browned and puffed, until browned and puffed, shifting the sheets from top to bottom and front to back halfway through.

Store them in an air tight plastic freezer container until ready to serve.

Sweet Strawberry And Pistachio Cookies

Nutrition Facts
Serving Size 20 g

Amount Per Serving
Calories 14 — Calories from Fat 9
% Daily Value*
Total Fat 1.0g — 1%
Cholesterol 36mg — 12%
Sodium 45mg — 2%
Potassium 13mg — 0%
Total Carbohydrates 0.2g — 0%
Protein 1.2g

Vitamin A 1% • Vitamin C 0%
Calcium 1% • Iron 1%

Nutrition Grade B-
* Based on a 2000 calorie diet

Prep time: 15 minutes
Cook time: 12 minutes
Total time: 27 minutes
Yield: 36 servings
INGREDIENTS
1 1/4 cups granulated sugar
1/2 cup brown sugar
1/2 cup unsalted butter, softened
1 teaspoon vanilla extract
1 large egg
7.9 ounces (about 1 3/4 cups) all-purpose flour
1 teaspoon baking soda
1/4 teaspoon salt
1 teaspoon black pepper
1/2 cup chopped dried strawberries
1/4 cup finely chopped pistachios
Parchment paper

INSTRUCTIONS

1. Preheat oven to 350 Fahrenheit. Blend granulated sugar, brown sugar, butter, and vanilla in a large bowl; beat with a mixer at moderate speed until fluffy. Combine egg; whisk just until combined. Whisk in flour, baking soda, and salt.

2. Blend black pepper into cookie dough at moderate speed. Mix in straw-berries and pistachios. Drop dough by tablespoonful 2 inches apart on parchment paper-lined baking sheets.

3 .Bake 10 to 12 minutes or until lightly browned.
Place cookies in a freezer air tight bag or container.

Pros for Freezing Meals

Time - I have to admit that at the outset my main reason for adopting the freezer meal system was to gain for myself some space and time. I realized that by stocking up my freezer with ready-cooked meals, my days, apart from the few each month spent cooking, would be much less hectic and I could actually find hours to follow non-domestic pursuits.

Money - It didn't take long for me to understand that by planning the meals and making strict ingredient lists that I was saving money. No more impulse buying, no more ordering a take-away because I just couldn't be bothered to cook and no more food wastage. Now everything I buy is used almost immediately while it is still fresh and full of vitamins. Gone are the days of throwing out dodgy meat or wilted vegetables because I didn't get around to using them before they expired!

Stress – There are those days when everything that can go wrong just does. The very last thing you feel like doing is even thinking about what to cook for the evening meal; then you remember that it really doesn't matter. All you have to do is take a chicken casserole from the freezer, pop it into the crockpot and just forget it until dinner time. Oh joy!

Weight Loss – The most incredible spin-off from my frozen meal idea is the weight loss I've achieved since starting the system two years ago. I don't have to feel deprived or hungry – I can eat as much as I like. All I have to do is follow my own guidelines for healthy family meals.

Tips for Freezing

Here are a few basic but vital tips to help you achieve successful results.

- Never re-freeze anything that has already been frozen before

Most prepared meals may be cooked from frozen: soups, casseroles, bakes, gratins and potato-topped pies are fine to cook straight from frozen. Use a lower temperature to start with, increasing the heat as the food begins to thaw

- Certain foods should never be cooked straight from frozen: these are raw chicken/turkey and joints of meat
- Always make sure anything you've prepared is completely cool before it goes into the freezer
- Put meals into sealed containers of sufficient grade to prevent the food spoiling in the freezer
- Label every dish carefully. You may think you'll remember what is in every container but believe me, you won't. Use a freezer-proof marker pen and always put the date on the label
- Work out how much food you need in each container. Better to be able to take out two smaller containers than to have to waste half of what you have put in one large one. Remember, you can only re-heat frozen food once
- For best results use only very fresh ingredients. Cool the cooked meals as quickly as possible and get them into the freezer the moment they are completely cool

- It is more cost effective to keep your freezer as full as possible because the cold air doesn't have to circulate so much thereby using less power

- If you have a power cut or if the freezer has been accidentally turned off, don't open the door. Food will remain frozen for about 24 hours if you keep the freezer firmly closed

What to Freeze
- Cheeses and butter freeze well
- Batch cooked dishes
- Soups and casseroles
- Home-made baby foods
- Fruit puree
- Bread
- Milk will freeze for one month. Defrost in the fridge and shake well before using
- Raw pastry – it takes about one hour to thaw

What Not to Freeze

- Vegetables with high water content like bean sprouts, cucumber, radishes
- Raw or hardboiled eggs
- Soft herbs like parsley, basil and chives
- Mayonnaise - it will split
- Plain yogurt, low-fat cream cheese and cottage cheese, in fact any low fat dairy will become watery if frozen.

Defrosting Tips

- The safest method of defrosting is to put the frozen items into the fridge. This is particularly important in the case of meat. Place frozen food on a tray at the bottom of the fridge and leave overnight or during the day.
- Remember not to put the frozen foods at the back of the fridge where it is coldest.
- It is possible to submerge food to be defrosted in cold water. The water must be changed every 30 minutes to make sure it doesn't begin to warm up because this could make bacteria grow in the food.
- The microwave is the fastest method of defrosting but it is not always even. Food can begin to cook on the outside, leaving the inside still frozen. Also, microwaves tend to make foods dry out so it's best to only use in a dire emergency.

Chapter 2: Recipes

Breakfasts

Here are some great instant breakfasts for those days when time is running away with you. They are full of slow-release, high energy nourishment but have very little saturated fat or refined sugar.

Nutty Banana Cookies

Ingredients: (24 cookies)
- 1 cup nut butter – smooth or chunky
- 4 ripe bananas – mashed
- 2½ cups oats
- 1 cup whole wheat flour
- ½ cup non-fat milk powder
- ½ tsp baking soda
- 1 cup runny honey

Instructions:
1. Preheat oven to 350 degrees. Line four baking sheets with non-stick parchment.
2. In a large bowl, mix nut butter, mashed banana and honey
3. In separate bowl mix together oats, flour, milk powder and baking soda.
4. Stir oat mixture into nut and banana mixture until thoroughly combined.

5. With a tablespoon, drop mounds of dough 2 inches apart onto the baking sheets. Flatten each mound slightly (they will spread a little anyway as they cook).

6. Bake for 10 to 15 minutes, or until golden. Allow to cool a little then carefully transfer to a cooling rack.

7. When they are completely cold, pack into plastic freezer boxes and freeze for up to 2 months.

Thaw completely before serving.

Oatmeal Brownies

Ingredients: (16 brownies)
- 6 cups of oats
- 4 teaspoons baking powder
- 1½ teaspoons salt
- ½ cup cocoa powder
- 1 teaspoon cinnamon
- ½ cup dark brown sugar
- ½ cup runny honey
- 4 tablespoons of either almond, coconut or walnut oil
- 1 cup pumpkin puree
- 2 cups skimmed milk
- 4 eggs
- 2 teaspoons vanilla extract

Instructions:
1. Preheat oven to 350 degrees.
2. Mix together oats, baking powder, salt, cocoa powder, cinnamon, brown sugar.
3. In a separate bowl whisk together honey, oil, pumpkin, milk, eggs and vanilla extract.
4. Add the liquid mixture into the dry mixture and mix well.
5. Pour the mixture into a two 9 x 13 baking pans.
6. Bake for 20 minutes or until firm to the touch.
7. Cool completely before cutting into squares.

Freeze in plastic lidded boxes for up to two months – thaw before serving.

Ham And Cheese Muffins

Ingredients: (24 muffins)
- 4 slices of ham
- 2 cups of grated cheese
- 16 eggs
- 4 slices of wholemeal bread, broken up into chunks
- 1 cup of skimmed milk
- 4 teaspoons mustard powder
- 2 teaspoons ground pepper

Instructions:
1. Preheat oven to 400 degrees.
2. Lightly grease muffin tins (use low fat spray if possible).
3. Place chunks of bread evenly into the muffin tins so that they fill about half of each tin.
4. Sprinkle a little cheese over the bread.
5. Add ham pieces evenly to each tin.
6. Whisk together eggs, mustard powder and pepper.
7. Pour egg mixture into each muffin tin so that it completely covers the layers of bread, ham and cheese. Don't fill it completely to the top or it may overflow in cooking.
8. Sprinkle more grated cheese on the top of each muffin.
9. Bake for 20 minutes until golden brown on top and cooked through the middle.

Allow to cool completely before freezing.

Re-heat straight from the freezer. Microwave for 30 seconds, turn over and microwave for a further 30 seconds.

Chocolate Banana Waffles

These are just such a treat! And as well as being delicious they're low in sugar and fat, full of healthy vitamins and take no time at all to make.

Ingredients: (16 waffles)
- 1 cup of white flour
- ½ cup of whole wheat flour
- ¼ cup of wheat germ
- ¾ cup of cocoa powder
- 3 tablespoons granulated sugar (or substitute sweetener)
- 3 tablespoons baking powder
- ¼ teaspoon salt
- 1¾ cups skimmed milk
- 2 ripe, mashed bananas
- 2 eggs, beaten
- ¼ cup canola oil
- 1 teaspoon vanilla extract

Instructions:
1. Preheat waffle iron.
2. Whisk together flours, what germ, cocoa, sugar or sweetener, baking powder and salt in a large bowl.
3. In a separate bowl, mix together milk, bananas, eggs, canola oil and vanilla extract until combined. Add this mixture to the dry ingredients and stir together until you have a smooth batter.
4. Coat the hot waffle iron with non-stick cooking spray and pour batter onto the waffle iron – approximately 2 cups. Cook on a medium-high setting.

5. Repeat until all the batter is used.

NOTE: These are great served with sliced bananas or maple syrup

Midday Meals

I've always believed that a satisfying lunch is a vital part of the day. It needs to be energy boosting and nutritious but not so heavy that it knocks you out for the afternoon. I think these fill the bill.

Honey Glazed Chicken

Hot tip – remove skin from chicken before cooking. It's the only fatty part of the meat and once it's cooked you might just be tempted to eat it!

Ingredients: (8 servings)
- 16 fresh chicken thighs
- 8 tablespoons of wholegrain mustard
- 8 tablespoons of clear honey

Instructions:
1. Preheat oven to 375 degrees.
2. Put chicken thighs in single layer in roasting pan.
3. Mix together mustard and honey, season with salt and pepper and brush mixture over chicken thighs.
4. Cook for 25-30 minutes, basting the chicken with pan juices occasionally until cooked through.

5. To freeze: Allow chicken pieces to cool completely then pack in freezer containers. They will be fine in the freezer for up to 2 months.

Defrost in the fridge overnight and then re-heat thoroughly in the oven (at least 20 minutes). Test they are completely hot right through by inserting a metal skewer right into one of the pieces and leaving it there for a few seconds. Remove and press the skewer to the inside of your wrist to check if it feels hot.

Roasted Golden Vegetable Soup

Ingredients: (16-20 servings)
- 2 large butternut squash
- 4 red peppers
- 4 yellow peppers
- 4 orange peppers
- 4 large red onions
- 6 large beefsteak tomatoes
- 8 garlic cloves
- Juice of 2 lemons
- A couple of sprigs of fresh rosemary
- 8 pints chicken stock
- 4 tbsp olive oil

Instructions:
1. Preheat the oven to 400 degrees.
2. Halve squash and scoop out seeds. Cut each half into four equal pieces.
3. Halve and de-seed peppers and cut into pieces.
4. Peel onions and cut into thick chunks.
5. Cut tomatoes into halves.
6. Arrange vegetables on large non-stick baking sheets.
7. Peel garlic and slice then tuck in between vegetables.
8. Sprinkle juice of lemons over vegetables and season well.
9. Brush olive oil all over vegetables. By brushing instead of pouring you will not use too much!
10. Bake for 30 minutes.
11. Discard rosemary, scrape flesh from the squash and place in a food processor or blender.

12. Add all other vegetables along with about ½ pint of chicken stock and process until smooth.
Transfer to a large pan and stir in remaining stock. Heat through for 5 minutes until piping hot.

The soup is now ready. Pour into containers and cool completely before sealing and freezing.

Corny Tuna Fritters

Ingredients: (24 servings)
- 2 x 400g cans sweetcorn
- 2 x 198g cans tuna in spring water or brine
- 6 medium potatoes
- Salt and pepper
- Fresh coriander
- 2 eggs - lightly beaten
- Olive oil

Instructions:
1. Preheat oven to 160 degrees.
2. Place drained tuna and sweetcorn into a large mixing bowl.
3. Put potatoes (unpeeled) into a pan of boiling water and simmer for about 12-15 minutes – don't let them cook too much. Drain and let them cool then peel with a sharp knife. Coarsely grate the potatoes into the sweetcorn and tuna mixture.
4. Add chopped coriander and season well.
5. Mix together all ingredients then divide mixture into 24 portions.
6. Shape each portion into a flat cake and place onto baking trays lined with non-stick parchment.
7. Brush with olive oil and bake for 15-20 minutes, until they are lightly golden.

Allow to cool completely before freezing.

Hot Tip: It's a good idea to put a small sheet of non-stick parchment between each fritter in the freezer container to prevent them sticking together.

Bake from frozen when required.

Pepper Stuffed Meatloaf

Ingredients: (Makes 2 loaves, each serving 4)
- 3 lb extra lean minced beef
- 2 onions
- Freshly chopped parsley
- Salt and ground black pepper
- 2 egg yolks
- 1 jar of preserved red pepper slices

Instructions:
1. Preheat oven to 375 degrees.
2. Brush 2 loaf tins with olive oil.
3. Peel and finely chop onion and place in a bowl with minced beef, 4 tbsp chopped parsley, egg yolks and seasoning. Mix well.
4. Divide mixture into quarters and press one quarter into each of the two tins. Make a lengthwise indent down the centre and lay the slices of red pepper along the length of mixture.
5. Top with the remaining meat, pressing down well.
6. Cover with baking parchment, then foil and bake for one hour or until juices run clear when a skewer is inserted into loaf.
7. Stand loaves for ten minutes, then drain away any juices.
8. This dish is great eaten cold with salad and pickles but may also be served hot with vegetables.

Loaves may be frozen but should be completely thawed before either re-heating or serving cold.

Evening Meals

This is the time of day when it's most likely for the family to eat together so here are a few of our family favourites. Apart from deciding which one to take out of the freezer in the morning, all I have to do is to cook some fresh green vegetables or maybe put together a big bowl of salad. Easy!

Fish Pie

Ingredients: (24 servings)
- 2kg **fresh** white fish
- 3kg potatoes, peeled and cut into chunks
- Salt and pepper
- 1.5ltr fish stock (make this up from stock pots or cubes)
- 3 onions, peeled and quartered
- 12 whole cloves
- 6 bay leaves
- Large bunch of chopped parsley
- 600g canned sweetcorn, drained
- 6 level tbsp vegetable gravy granules
- Freshly grated nutmeg
- 3 eggs, beaten

Instructions:
1. Boil potatoes in pan of lightly salted water for about 20 minutes, until tender. Drain and mash with 300ml of the fish stock. Set aside and keep warm.

2.Put fish in a large saucepan with remaining fish stock. Stud each onion quarter with a clove and add them to the stock, also add the bay leaves. Bring gently to the boil and reduce to a simmer for 8-10 minutes.

3. Remove the fish onto a large plate and strain stock into a jug to cool.

4. Flake fish into bite size chunks and divide equally between 3 foil baking dishes. On top of fish, scatter the parsley and sweetcorn.

To make sauce, return the fish stock to the pan and bring it to the boil then slmmer for 8 minutes, stirring continuously. Add vegetable gravy granules and continue to stir over gentle heat until sauce thickens. Add salt, pepper and nutmeg then pour sauce equally over the three lots of fish mixture.

5. Preheat oven to 200 degrees.

6. Divide mashed potato to top each pie. Fluff up potato topping then brush all over with beaten egg.

7. Bake for 30 minutes until lightly golden.

Cool completely before putting on lids and freezing.

Chicken And Pumpkin Pot Roast

Ingredients: (4 servings)
- 4 chicken breasts or leg portions or thighs (skinned)
- Salt and ground black pepper
- 1 tsp olive oil
- 3 garlic cloves - peeled & chopped
- 2 onions – peeled & sliced
- 454g pumpkin – flesh cut into 25cm chunks
- 2 x 397g cans chopped tomatoes
- 2 bay leaves
- 2 courgettes – thickly sliced
- 1 yellow pepper – thickly sliced

Instructions:

1. In non-stick pan, brushed with olive oil, sear chicken on all sides.
2. Into a large Le Crueset-style pan put onion, garlic and pumpkin. Add tomatoes and chicken, bring to the boil. Put lid on pan and simmer for 30 minutes.
3. Add courgettes and pepper. Simmer for another 20 minutes until chicken is cooked through.

NOTE: This dish may be transferred for freezing into a large foil baking dish with lid. I find it easier to cook one family sized portion at a time as my cast iron cooking pot will only comfortably take four chicken breast portions plus all the vegetables!

Saucy Meatballs

Ingredients: (makes 60 small meatballs – use either extra lean minced beef, lamb, chicken or pork)
- 1.5kg extra lean minced meat
- 12 scallions
- 3 tsp dried mixed herbs
- Salt and pepper
- 3 finely chopped onions
- 3 yellow peppers
- 3 courgettes
- 2 egg plants
- 3 bay leaves
- 3 x 397g cans chopped tomatoes with garlic chopped parsley

Instructions:
1. Finely chop scallions, place in mixing bowl and add meat, dried herbs and plenty of seasoning.
2. Mix together well then form into 60 small balls. Put them on a tray lined with baking parchment, cover and chill for 30 minutes.
3. To make the sauce, place in a large saucepan chopped onion, pepper, courgettes and egg plants. Add bay leaves and chopped tomatoes. Season well and bring to the boil, turn down heat and simmer for about 10 minutes until vegetables are just tender.
4. Preheat the broiler to a medium setting then arrange meatballs onto the rack and cook for 8-10 minutes, turning frequently. They should look golden brown

when ready but try cutting one in half to check! Allow all juices/fat to completely drain away.

5. To serve at once, simply re-heat the sauce and pour some into a serving dish and pile the meatballs in the middle of the sauce, sprinkled with chopped parsley.

6. To freeze - pour sauce into foil or plastic containers and pack meatballs in separately container. When completely cold, put on lids and freeze. May be re-heated straight from frozen or from thawed.

Bobotie

This is an adaptation of a South African dish. It is almost a cross between Shepherd's Pie but with the Greek method of adding beaten egg and milk as a topping. It's a real favourite!

Ingredients: (makes 3 dishes, each serving 4 people)
- 1.5kg extra lean minced beef or lamb
- 3 finely chopped onions
- 2 tbsp olive oil
- 255g whole wheat breadcrumbs
- 255g raisins
- 255g roasted peanuts or cashew nuts (optional)
- 6 tbsp mild curry powder
- Juice of 2 lemons
- 6 tbsp mango chutney
- 12 eggs
- 1.5 pint semi-skimmed milk
- 3 bay leaves

Instructions:

1. Put meat into a large bowl and season generously with salt and freshly ground pepper, then set aside.
2. Fry onions lightly in olive oil and stir in curry powder or paste. When aromatic remove from heat.
3. Add breadcrumbs and mix well then add raisins, nuts, lemon juice, chutney and seasoning then add to the meat mixture and mix very thoroughly.
4. When mixture is cold, add six lightly beaten eggs and mix some more until everything is combined.
5. Turn mixture into 3 ovenproof dishes – these may be foil baking dishes with lids for the freezer.
6. Put a couple of bay leaves on top of each dish and cook in a moderate oven for 35 minutes.
7. While this is cooking, beat remaining 6 eggs with milk, salt and pepper.
8. At the end of the 35 minute cooking time, remove the dishes from the oven, discard the bay leaves and pour egg and milk over the top of each.
9. Return to the oven for a further 35 minutes or until the egg mixture has set and is a light golden brown. When lightly pressed the topping should be firm, not runny.

Cool completely before putting lids on dishes and freezing.

Part 2

Introduction

You are at a point in life when you know you need to make some healthy choices especially when it comes to your choice of food. The only problem is you can't seem to spare any minute to cook a nice and healthy meal when you get back home from work. The result? Takeout that you are genuinely so fed up of taking but the mere thought of fighting with pans and pots in your kitchen is almost unfathomable after a long and tedious day at work.

Well, this is where our Crockpot/ Slow Cooker Freezer Recipes come in. This book is here to show you that it is actually possible for you to make the healthiest meals for your family without breaking a sweat. It's as easy as combining all the ingredients of your meal in your slow cooker in the morning before you go to work and on coming home, voila! You have a hot and tasty dish ready and waiting.

Sounds too good to be true? Well, we haven't even gotten to the best part! You can prepare and cook all your meals in advance, say during the weekend or when you have some free time and once your food is ready, let it cool and pack it in your freezer. Come weekday, all you will need to do is take out your food, thaw it and you have a beautiful home cooked dinner. Forget about the frozen food from your supermarket, you can now make your own.

We will start by teaching you the basics of using a crockpot and why you need to have one, if you don't already have one; best food freezing and defrosting practices then jump right into yummy and healthy recipes that you can make for your family stress free.

Now, get your reading glasses, put your apron on standby and let's get into this cooking adventure!

Why You Need The Crockpot Miracle In Your Home

Ever dreamt of coming home to an aromatic home with a steaming hot meal only waiting to be served after a long day at work? Well, the crockpot is the surest way to make your dream come true! Forget about running around like crazy like a headless chicken trying to find the right ingredients and whipping them up together to make a decent meal for dinner when your shoulders can barely stay upright because of how tired you are. We are talking about, throwing in all your ingredients in one cooker before you prepare to leave for work in the morning and coming back home to the yummiest, well done meal in the evening!

Here are some more benefits of cooking using a crockpot that will have you going to buy one immediately after this if you don't already have one.

• Delicious and nutritious dishes

Usually, meats and fresh vegetables are cooked in a crockpot for many hours than usual, at a low temperature. As a result, nutrition-packed juices from the meats and veggies are released and retained as there is no escape through steam meaning you get the best of flavors and nutrients.

• Saves a lot of your time

Perhaps the most attractive thing about using a crockpot is the fact that you are not going crazy in the kitchen over a pot of food, checking it after every few minutes so it doesn't burn. The only thing you may have to do with a slow cooker, especially if you are cooking meat, is to brown it in some oil over a stove top, if you want to have some great color in your stew then throw in all the ingredients in your slow cooker and come back to it once the cooking hours are done. Additionally, if you stay out longer than the cook time, your crockpot automatically shifts to warm mode so you still have a hot meal to come back home to!

Timeless

A crockpot is one of the kitchen equipment you can use all year round for many years to come and is not just limited to hot bowls of soup and stews for winter. You can also use a slow cooker to make yummy desserts and casseroles to be enjoyed during the summer with the beauty being you can use it in place of the oven during summer so you don't make an already sweltering kitchen hotter than it already is. Or, better still, you can leave a casserole or meal of choice cooking as you go have fun at the beach, or somewhere else cooler then come back to a ready meal.

• Easy to freeze

Most meals that are cooked in a crockpot can be easily packed and stored in your freezer to be eaten at a later date; saving you even more time.

Great Tips For Using Your Crockpot

• Prep in advance

If your mornings are usually busy, prepare everything that you are going to need for your meal the night before. That is, chop your meats and veggies, if using, then store in your crockpot's dish and store in the refrigerator overnight. However, if you are using a combination of both meat and veggies, store them separately to avoid any chance of contamination.

When using a crockpot, your ingredients should ideally be at room temperature, or as close to it as possible. So, you can take out your ingredients from the fridge, immediately you get up in the morning and leave them to warm up for about 20-30 minutes before turning on your crockpot.

• Trim excess fat

The beauty of using a crockpot is you don't need to add any oil to your meals, especially if they are meat based. They won't stick to the bottom for as long as there is enough moisture in the in the cooker. Usually when you cook meat on the stove top, the fat tends to drain away on its own but this is not the case in a crockpot and if you don't trim off the excess fat, you may end up with pools of oil in your stew.

For a tastier and healthier result, trim off the excess fat.

• Go easy on the soup

When cooking using a slow cooker, the moisture doesn't evaporate since it cooks with a tightly sealed lid all through. When adapting a recipe that's typically cooked on stove top, it's advisable to reduce the liquid content by about a third. As a rule of thumb, the soup/liquid should only just cover the ingredients. Otherwise, overfilling your crockpot with soup or liquid may lead to a leakage from the top and risk your food not cooking as well as it should.

When filling your crockpot with ingredients, don't go past the three quarter-way mark.

• Thickening your sauce

The fact that soup doesn't easily reduce in a crockpot means that it also doesn't thicken. If you like your broth or sauces nice and thick, you can roll your meat chunks in flour before browning them and adding them to the crockpot or alternatively, you can add a bit of cornstarch-water mixture towards the end of your cooking. Add it within the last 5-10 minutes of cook time.

• Don't be a peeping Tom

Crockpots are designed to do their own thing. All you need to do is add all your ingredients, seal the lid, turn it on and leave it to cook for the required number of hours. If you keep checking the progress of your meal by the hour then you are going to have to increase your cook time as every time you take out the lid, you release some heat. Needless to say, your meal won't be as glorious as it would have been had you trusted the crockpot to do its thing!

• When to add ingredients

The best crockpot recipes, like the ones we are going to share in our next section, are those where most of the ingredients are added at the beginning of the cooking process. This leaves you with a lot of time to do your other things.

However, if a meal calls for pasta, rice, fresh herbs or slightly cooked veggies, these you are going to add towards the end of your cooking.

How do you know how long you should cook a meal?
If a meal typically takes:

§ 15 to 30 minutes to cook, then cook it for 1 to 2 hours on the High setting or 4 to 6 hours on the low setting

§ 30 minutes to 1 hour to cook, then cook it for 2 to 3 hours on the high setting or 5 to 7 hours on the low setting

§ 1 to 2 hours to cook, then cook it for 3 to 4 hours on the high setting or 6 to 8 hours on the low setting

§ 2 to 4 hours to cook, then cook it for 4-6 hours on the high setting or 8-12 hours on the low setting

Safety Tips When Freezing And Defrosting Food

When it comes to freezing and defrosting, avoiding contamination is the most important thing. Here are some great tips that will guide you on how to freeze and defrost your food and also on the best foods to freeze and those not to freeze.

• Let foods cool completely

Freezing hot foods increases your freezer's temperature which could cause the other foods in the freezer to start defrosting, therein increasing risk of cross-contamination.

• You can only refreeze pre-frozen food if you are planning to cook in between

When you thaw food, bacteria can easily multiply especially when the food achieves room temperature. If you return it to the freezer, most of the bacteria survives and in the event you do a second thawing, the bacterial levels can become harmful. But one the other hand if you cook the food between thawing, for example, thawing ground beef, turning it into a casserole and freezing it once its cooked and cooled then it's no problem as the bacteria will have been destroyed when cooking.

• It's more economical to run a full freezer

This is because the cool air does not need to make too many circulations meaning it uses less power. It is therefore advisable to freeze most of your food to save on power and also time.

• Measure your portions

Freeze your food in portions that are realistic for you and your family. Freezing extremely large portions is not advisable as it means you are going to have to refreeze your food which can give room to bacterial contamination.

- When not sure, you are safer throwing it out

Contrary to popular opinion, freezing your food does not kill bacteria. If you feel unsure of the condition of the food you froze or are not sure of how long a particular food has been in the freezer, you are better off tossing it out than eating it and getting sick.

- Freeze fresh food

The thing about freezing is that it does not improve the quality of your food. What this means is that if you freeze fresh food, then you are going to get fresh tasting food after thawing but if on the other hand you freeze not-so-fresh food, then what you get after thawing will taste exactly the same.

- Label your food

As a rule of thumb, label your frozen food and indicate the date of freezing so you are able to keep track of what is in your freezer and when you should eat it.

- Defrost your freezer every now and then

If your freezer becomes icy then it comes less efficient. Make it a rule to defrost your freezer if ice builds up. Don't worry about your frozen food as most foods will remain frozen for up to 24 hours.

- In the event of a power outage...

Refrain from opening your freezer door so your food can remain frozen for up to 24 hours, leaving you with enough time to sort out the power problem.

Foods that are great to freeze

§ Margarine and butter can be frozen for up to 3 months.

§ Most bread varieties apart from crusty breads can stay frozen for up to 3 months.

§ Shredded cheese can be frozen for up to 4 months and you can use it immediately you take it out without having to wait for it to thaw.

§ Pastry (raw) can freeze for up to 6 months.

§ Milk can stay frozen for up to a month.

Foods that should not be frozen

§ Hard boiled eggs become rubbery when frozen.

§ Raw eggs when frozen crack.

§ Veggies with a high water content such as cucumber and radishes become limp after being frozen.

§ Fresh herbs when frozen are only great for stews but not garnishes.

§ Cottage cheese, plain yogurt and single cream become runny when frozen.

Slow Cooker Chillis

Paleo Jalapeno Chili

Yield: 6 servings
Total Time: 4 Hours 25 Minutes
Prep Time: 25 Minutes
Cook Time: 4 Hours

Ingredients
- 1-1.5 pounds ground beef/chicken/turkey
- 1 red bell pepper, chopped
- 1 green bell pepper, chopped
- 2 jalapeños, finely diced
- 1 acorn squash, peeled and diced
- 2 zucchini, sliced
- 4 small carrots, sliced
- 3 green onions, thinly sliced
- 1 (28 ounce) can whole peeled tomatoes
- 4 tbsp. chili powder
- 1 (6 ounce) can tomato paste
- 1 (14 ounce) can tomato sauce

Instructions

1. Brown the meat in a pan over medium heat. 5-8 minutes.
2. Chop the vegetables and add to the slow cooker. Remove the ribs and seeds from the Jalapeños and add with the rest.
3. Add the whole tomatoes and break up with a spatula.
4. Stir in the chili powder and other remaining ingredients.
5. Cook on low for about 5 hours.

Sweet Potato Chili

Yield: 10 Servings
Total Time: 7 Hours 10 Minutes
Prep Time: 10 Minutes
Cook Time: 7 Hours

Ingredients
- 2 pounds ground beef
- 3 cups beef stock
- 2 sweet potatoes, peeled and diced
- 1 clove garlic, minced
- 1 onion, diced
- 1 (14-oz) can petite minced tomatoes
- 2 (14-oz) cans tomato sauce
- 3-4 tbsp. chili powder
- ¼ tsp. oregano
- 2 tsp. salt
- ½ tsp. black pepper
- Cilantro, optional, for garnish

Directions
1. Brown the beef in a pan over medium heat. 5-8 minutes.
2. Drain the excess fat and transfer to the slow cooker.

3. Stir in the remaining ingredients.
4. Cook on low for about 7 hours.
5. Optional – garnish with cilantro when serving.

Best Ever Crock Pot Chili

Yield: 4-6 Servings
Total Time: 6 Hours 30 Minutes
Prep Time: 30 Minutes
Cook Time: 6 Hours
Ingredients
Seasoning Mix
- 4 tbsp. chili powder
- ½ tsp. cayenne pepper
- 1 tsp. oregano
- 1 ½ tsp. garlic powder
- 2 ½ tsp. ground cumin
- 2 ½ tsp. ground coriander

Chili
- 1 ½ pounds ground beef
- 1 tbsp. minced onion
- 2 (15 ounce) cans kidney beans
- 1 (15 ounce) can tomato sauce
- 1 (28 ounce) can diced tomatoes

Directions

1. In a small bowl mix the seasoning. Don't panic – you're only going to use all small amount this time. Store the rest in an airtight container for the future.
2. In a large skillet set over medium heat, brown the ground beef; stir in about 3 teaspoons of the seasoning and onions until well combined.
3. In the slow cooker add 1 can of the beans, tomato sauce, tomatoes, and 2 teaspoons of the seasoning.
4. Process the remaining beans in a blender until very smooth; add to the slow cooker and add meat mixture.
5. Stir and cook, covered, on low for about 6 hours.

Pork & Black Bean Chili

Yield: 6-8 Servings
Total Time: 9 Hours 20 Minutes
Prep Time: 20 Minutes
Cook Time: 9 Hours

Ingredients

- 3 pounds boneless pork ribs, diced
- 3 tbsp. all-purpose flour
- 1 1/2 tsp. ground cumin
- 2 tsp. salt
- 2 tsp. ground black pepper
- 1/4 cup vegetable oil
- 2 cups diced white onion
- 2 (15-oz.) cans black beans, drained and rinsed
- 3/4 cup chicken broth
- 3 cups chopped poblano peppers
- 9 medium tomatillos, diced
- 3 garlic cloves, minced
- 1 1/2 tbsp. chili powder
- 1 1/2 tbsp. dried oregano
- 2 tbsp. plain cornmeal
- Chipotle Cream to serve

Directions

1. In a large bowl, stir together flour, cumin, salt and black pepper until well combined; toss with pork until well coated.

2. Sauté the pork in oil for about 10 minutes or until browned and then transfer to the slow cooker.

3. Stir in the remaining ingredients except cornmeal and cook, covered, on low for about 8 hours.

4. Stir in cornmeal and continue cooking for 1 hour more.

5. Serve the chilli with Chipotle Cream.

Turkey Chili

Yield: 4-6 Servings
Total Time: 4 Hours 10 Minutes
Prep Time: 10 Minutes
Cook Time: 4 Hours

Ingredients

- 1 1/4 pounds lean ground turkey
- 1 garlic clove, minced
- 1 large red onion, chopped
- 1 (15-oz.) can black beans
- 1 (8-oz.) can tomato sauce
- 1 (28-oz.) can crushed tomatoes
- 1 green bell pepper, chopped
- 1 red bell pepper, chopped
- 1 1/2 cups frozen corn kernels
- 1 package (1 1/4-oz.) chili seasoning mix
- 1/2 tsp. sea salt

Directions

1. In a large skillet, cook ground turkey, garlic and onion until turkey is no longer pink.

2. Transfer the mixture to a slow cooker and stir in the remaining ingredients.

3. Cook, covered, on high for about 4 hours. Serve hot with your favorite toppings.

Easy Crockpot Chili

Yield: 6-8 Servings
Total Time: 6 Hours 10 Minutes
Prep Time: 10 Minutes
Cook Time: 6 Hours

Ingredients

- 1 1/2 pounds lean ground beef
- 1 onion, chopped
- 1 small green bell pepper, chopped
- 2 garlic cloves, minced
- 2 (16-ounce) cans red kidney beans, rinsed and drained
- 2 (14-1/2-ounce) cans diced tomatoes
- 2 to 3 tablespoons chili powder
- 1 tsp. salt
- 1 tsp. pepper
- 1 tsp. ground cumin

Directions

1. In a large skillet set over medium high heat, cook ground beef, garlic, onion, and green bell pepper until beef is no longer pink.

2. Transfer the mixture to a slow cooker and stir in the remaining ingredients; cook, covered, on low for about 6 hours.

Thai Red Curry With Kabocha Squash

Yield: 4 to 6 Servings
Total Time: 3 Hours 45 Minutes
Prep Time: 45 Minutes
Cook Time: 3 Hours

Ingredients

- 3 pounds squash, peeled, seeded, and diced
- 1 tbsp. vegetable oil
- 1 medium red onion, diced
- 1 tbsp. ginger, grated
- 4 medium garlic cloves, chopped
- 2 medium green bell peppers, cut into 1/4-inch strips
- 1 1/2 tsp. salt
- 1/2 cup water
- 2 cups coconut milk
- 3 tbsp. Thai red curry paste
- 1 tbsp. soy sauce
- 1/4 cup chopped cilantro
- 2 tsp. freshly squeezed lime juice

- Steamed cooked brown rice, for serving

Directions

1. In a large pan, heat oil until hot, but not smoking; stir in onion and a teaspoon of salt; cook for about 6 minutes or until onion is tender.
2. Stir in ginger, garlic and peppers and cook for 1 minute more or until fragrant.
3. Transfer to a slow cooker and stir in the remaining ingredients except lime juice and cilantro.
4. Cook, covered, on low for about 3 hours or until squash is tender.
5. Remove from heat and stir in lime juice and cilantro; serve hot over cooked rice.

Slow Cooker Seafood & Fish

Seafood Stew

Yield: 6 Servings
Total Time: 3 Hours 45 Minutes
Prep Time: 15 Minutes
Cook Time: 3 Hours 30 Minutes
Ingredients:

- 2 pounds seafood (1 pound large shrimp & 1 pound scallops)
- 1/2 cup chopped white onion
- 3 garlic cloves, minced
- 1 tbsp. tomato paste
- 1 can (28 oz) crushed tomatoes
- 4 cups vegetable broth
- 1 pound yellow potatoes, diced
- 1 tsp. dried basil
- 1 tsp. dried thyme
- 1 tsp. dried oregano
- 1/8 tsp. cayenne pepper
- 1/4 tsp. crush red pepper flakes
- 1/2 tsp. celery salt
- salt and pepper
- handful of chopped parsley

Directions:

1. Mix all ingredients, except seafood, into the slow cooker and cover; cook on high for about 2 hours or until potatoes are tender.
2. Stir in seafood and continue cooking for 30 minutes more or until seafood is cooked through.
3. Serve hot with crusty bread and garnished with parsley.

Coconut Curry Shrimp

Yield: 4 Servings
Total Time: 2 Hours 5 Minutes
Prep Time: 5 Minutes
Cook Time: 2 Hours

Ingredients
- 1 lb shrimp, with shells
- 15 ounces water
- 30 ounces light coconut milk
- ½ cup Thai red curry sauce
- ¼ cup cilantro
- 2½ tsp. lemon garlic seasoning

Directions
1. In a slow cooker, combine water, coconut milk, red curry paste, cilantro, and lemon garlic seasoning; stir to mix well and cook on high for about 2 hours.
2. Add shrimp and continue cooking for another 30 minutes or until shrimp is cooked through.
3. Serve garnished with cilantro.

Thai Seafood Boil

Yield: 4 Servings
Total Time: 4 Hours 10 Minutes
Prep Time: 10 Minutes
Cook Time: 4 Hours

Ingredients

- ½ pound snow crab
- ½ pound shrimp (in shells)
- 1 stalk lemongrass, outer layer and top inch removed
- 2 tsp ginger
- ¼ fresh mint, chopped
- 1 lime, cut in half
- 2 garlic cloves, minced
- 1 small onion, cut into quarters
- 2 cups coconut milk
- 32 ounces homemade broth
- ½ tsp. cumin
- 1 tsp. salt
- 1 celery stalks, cut into 1-inch pieces
- 1 pound sweet potatoes, cut into quarters

- 1 bell pepper, cut into 1-inch pieces
- 1 ear of corn, cut into 3-inch chunks

Directions

1. Smash the end of lemongrass stalk with a rolling pin until soft; transfer to a slow cooker along with ginger, mint, lime, garlic, onion, coconut milk, broth, cumin and salt.
2. Stir to combine well and then add in celery and sweet potatoes. Cook, covered, on high for about 2 hours.
3. Add corn and bell pepper and continue cooking for 1 hour more.
4. Stir in seafood and cook for about 20 minutes more.

Lemony Tilapia With Asparagus

Yield: 6 Servings
Total Time: 2 Hours 15 Minutes
Prep Time: 15 Minutes
Cook Time: 2 Hours

Ingredients

- 6 tilapia filets
- 1 bundle of asparagus
- 12 tbsp. lemon juice
- Lemon pepper seasoning
- 3 tbsp. melted butter

Directions

1. Divide the asparagus into equal amounts per each fillet.
2. Place each fillet in the center of a foil and sprinkle with about 1 tsp. of lemon pepper seasoning; drizzle with about 2 tbsp. of lemon juice and about ½ tbsp. melted butter.
3. Top each filet with the asparagus and fold the foil to form a packet.
4. Repeat with the remaining ingredients and then place the packets into a slow cooker.
5. Cook on high for about 2 hours

Citrus Tilapia

Yield: 4 Servings
Total Time: 2 Hours 10 Minutes
Prep Time: 10 Minutes
Cook Time: 2 Hours

Ingredients

- 4 tilapia filets

- 1 10-ounce can mandarin oranges

- 2 tbsp. garlic butter, diced into small pieces

- Sea salt and pepper

Directions

1. Arrange fish side by side onto a large piece of aluminum foil and sprinkle with garlic evenly.
2. Top the fish with oranges and season with salt and pepper; fold the foil to wrap the content well.
3. Place in the slow cooker and cook, covered, on high for about 2 hours.

Seafood Stew

Yield: 6-8 Servings
Total Time: 4 Hours 55 Minutes
Prep Time: 10 Minutes
Cook Time: 4 Hours 45 Minutes

Ingredients

- 1 6 1/2-ounce can clams with juice
- 3/4 pound medium shrimp, tails removed, shelled
- 1 pound cod filets, sliced into 1-inch pieces
- 2 cups chopped red onions
- 5 garlic cloves, minced
- 2 stalks celery, chopped
- 1 can diced tomatoes
- 1 28-ounce can diced tomatoes
- 1 tbsp. olive oil
- 1 tbsp. red wine vinegar
- 1/2 cup dry white wine or water
- 1/4 cup chopped fresh parsley
- 1/4 tsp. crushed red pepper flakes
- 1/4 tsp. sugar

- 2 1/2 tsp. lemon-pepper seasoning

Directions

1. Combine all ingredients, except seafood, in the slow cooker and cook on high for about 4 hours.
2. Add seafood and cover; cook for about 45 minutes or until fish flakes easily.

Shrimp Bisque

Yield: 6 Servings
Total Time: 4 Hours 45 Minutes
Prep Time: 15 Minutes
Cook Time: 4 Hours 30 Minutes

Ingredients

- 1 pound shrimp, peeled, deveined, and roughly chopped
- 3 tbsp. butter
- 3 cloves garlic, minced
- 2 medium leeks, chopped
- ¼ cup dry sherry
- 1 14 oz. can diced tomatoes
- ⅓ cup tomato paste
- 1½ cups corn
- 4 cups seafood stock
- 2 tsp. kosher salt
- 1 tsp. pepper
- 2 tsp old bay seasoning
- 1 cup heavy cream

- ¼ cup flour

Directions

1. In a large pan set over medium low heat, melt butter; stir in garlic and leeks and sauté for about 10 minutes or until translucent and tender.
2. Transfer the leek mixture to the slow cooker and stir in sherry, diced tomatoes, tomato paste, corn, seafood stock, salt, pepper and old bay. Cook on low for about 4 hours.
3. Transfer the mixture to a blender and puree until smooth; return to the slow cooker and stir in chopped shrimp, flour, and heavy cream. Continue cooking for about 30 minutes more or until shrimp is cooked through.

Spaghetti Squash Shrimp Scampi

Yield: 4 Servings
Total Time: 2 Hours 25 Minutes
Prep Time: 5 Minutes
Cook Time: 2 Hours 20 Minutes

Ingredients

- 3 pound spaghetti squash, halved crosswise and seeds removed
- 3/4 pound shrimp
- 32 ounces vegetable broth
- 1 tbsp. ghee
- 2½ tsp. lemon-garlic seasoning
- 1 red onion, chopped

Directions

1. Add vegetable broth to a slow cooker and stir in ghee, onion, and lemon garlic seasoning;
2. Add the spaghetti squash to the slow cooker, hollow side down.
3. Cook on high for about 2 hours.
4. Add shrimp and continue cooking for about 20 minutes more.

Lime Cilantro Fish Tacos

Yield: 6 Servings
Total Time: 4 Hours 10 Minutes
Prep Time: 10 Minutes
Cook Time: 4 Hours

Ingredients

- 6 frozen tilapia fillets, frozen
- 1/2 tsp. minced garlic
- 1 cup diced tomatoes
- 1 cup diced green chilies
- 1/4 cup fresh chopped cilantro
- 2 tbsp. fresh lime juice
- 1/4 tsp. sea salt
- 1/4 tsp. black pepper
- Soft taco shells to serve

Directions

1. Add the tilapia to a slow cooker and cover with the remaining ingredients, except taco shells;

2. Cook on low for about 4 hours.

3. Remove from heat and flake fish with a fork, mixing well with other ingredients.

4. Spoon the mixture into the taco shells and serve.

Greek Fish Stew

Yield: 5 Servings
Total Time: 5 Hours 10 Minutes
Prep Time: 10 Minutes
Cook Time: 5 Hours

Ingredients

- 5 large white fish fillets

- 1 large red onion, chopped

- 4 cloves of garlic

- 1 leek, sliced

- 1 carrot, chopped

- 3 sticks celery, chopped

- 1 can tomatoes

- 1/2 tsp. saffron threads

- 8 cups fish stock

- 2 tbsp. fresh lemon juice

- 1 tbsp. lemon zest

- handful parsley leaves chopped

- handful mint leaves chopped

Directions

1. Combine all ingredients in a slow cooker and cover. Cook on high for about 5 hours.

2. Serve with bread. That's all!

Soups, Stews & Curries

Fat Burner Veggie Soup

Yield: 8 Servings
Total Time: 7 Hours 20 Minutes
Prep Time: 20 Minutes
Cook Time: 7 Hours

Ingredients
- 4 cups navy beans
- 1 sweet potato, peeled, diced
- 1 clove garlic, minced
- 1 small yellow onion, diced
- 1 stalk celery, diced
- 3 carrots, peeled and sliced
- 1 tsp. paprika
- 1/8 tsp. allspice
- 1/2 tsp. black pepper
- ¼ tsp. sea salt
- 2 cups diced tomatoes
- 4 cups vegetable broth
- 1 bay leaf
- 4 cups baby spinach
- 1 tsp. extra-virgin olive oil
- 10 cups water

Directions
1. Combine all ingredients, except olive oil and spinach, in a slow cooker.

2. Cook, covered, for about 7 hours or until the vegetables are tender.
3. Remove the pot from heat and mash the ingredients with a fork.
4. Return to the pot and continue cooking for 1 hour more.
5. Stir in spinach and cook, for about 5 minutes or until wilted.
6. Serve drizzled with a splash of extra virgin olive oil. Enjoy!

French Onion Soup

Yield: 2 Servings
Total Time: 8 Hours 10 Minutes
Prep Time: 10 Minutes
Cook Time: 8 Hours

Ingredients
· 1/4 cup unsalted butter
· 1 bay leaf
· 6 thyme sprigs
· 1 tbsp. sugar
· 2 cups sliced sweet onion
· 2 tbsp. red wine vinegar
· 6 cups beef stock
· 1 1/2 tsp. kosher salt
· 1 tsp. black pepper
· 1 ¼ cups shredded Gruyere cheese

Directions
1. In a slow cooker, combine butter, bay leaf and thyme.
2. Add sugar and onions and cook, covered, on high for about 8 hours.
3. Discard bay leaf and thyme and stir in vinegar, stock, salt and pepper.
4. Continue cooking for about 30 minutes on high.

Detox Veggie Soup

Yield: 1 Serving
Total Time: 3 Hours 10 Minutes
Prep Time: 10 Minutes
Cook Time: 3 Hours

Ingredients

- 1 medium cauliflower
- 8 cups water
- 1 tsp. lemon juice
- 3 tsp. ground flax seeds
- 3 cups spinach
- 1 tsp. cayenne pepper
- 1 tsp. black pepper
- 1 tsp. soy sauce

Directions

1. Core cauliflower and cut the florets into large pieces; reserve stems for juicing.
2. Add cauliflower to a slow cooker and add water; cook on low for about 3 hours.
3. Transfer the cauliflower to a blender along with 2 cups of cooking liquid; blend until very smooth.
4. Add the remaining ingredients and continue blending until very smooth. Serve hot or warm.

Hot & Sour Flat-Belly Soup

Yield: 4 Servings
Total Time: 4 Hours 15 Minutes
Prep Time: 15 Minutes
Cook Time: 4 Hours

Ingredients
- 2 tbsp. extra-virgin olive oil
- 1 red onion, sliced
- 2 jalapeño peppers, seeds removed and diced
- 4 cups sliced green cabbage
- 1 carrot, peeled and chopped
- 4 cups crushed tomatoes
- 2 cup chicken breast, shredded
- 4 cup vegetable broth
- 3 tbsp. apple cider vinegar
- 2 tbsp. brown sugar
- ½ tsp. salt
- ¼ tsp. black pepper

Directions
1. Heat extra virgin olive oil in a pan set over medium heat; stirring red onion, jalapenos, cabbage, and carrot; sauté for about 7 minutes or until almost tender.
2. Transfer to a slow cooker and stir in tomatoes, chicken breast, broth, apple cider vinegar, and brown sugar, salt and pepper until well combined.
3. Cook on low for about 4 hours or until chicken shreds easily. Serve hot.

Spicy Green Soup

Yield: 2 Servings
Total Time: 3 Hours 15 Minutes
Prep Time: 15 Minutes
Cook Time: 3 Hours

Ingredients
- 1 cup chickpeas
- 1 green bell pepper, chopped
- 1 red onion, chopped
- 4 celery stalks, chopped
- 2 cups chopped spinach
- 1 tsp. dried mint
- 1/2 tsp. ground cumin
- 1/2 tsp. ground ginger
- 1/2 tsp. cardamom
- 2 cloves of garlic
- 1 tbsp. coconut milk
- sea salt and freshly ground black pepper

Directions

1. Combine all ingredients, except spinach and coconut milk, in a slow cooker; cook on low for about 3 hours or until chickpeas are tender.

2. Remove from heat and stir in spinach; let sit for about 5 minutes and then blend the mixture until very smooth.

3. Serve the soup into soup bowls and add coconut milk. Season with salt and more pepper and enjoy!

Red Onion & Apple Soup

Yield: 6 Servings
Total Time: 4 Hours 10 Minutes
Prep Time: 10 Minutes
Cook Time: 4 Hours

Ingredients
· 1 tbsp. canola oil
· 1 cup chopped red onion
· 3 organic apples, diced
· 8 cups vegetable broth
· 1/2 tbsp. chopped fresh rosemary
· 1 leek, chopped
· 1/2 tbsp. fresh thyme
· A pinch of cayenne pepper
· A pinch of sea salt

Directions
1. In a medium saucepan, heat canola oil; stir in onion and sauté for about 4 minutes or until fragrant and golden;
2. Transfer the sautéed onion to a slow cooker and stir in broth and bring the mixture to a gentle boil.
3. Stir in the apples, leek, thyme and rosemary; cook on low for about 4 hours.
4. Season with salt and pepper and serve.

Chipotle Black Bean Soup

Yield: 6 servings

Total Time: 3 Hours 10 Minutes
Prep Time: 20 Minutes
Cook Time: 3 Hours

Ingredients
- 1 tbsp. extra virgin olive oil
- 1 medium green bell pepper, chopped
- 1 medium red bell pepper, chopped
- 2 medium red onions, chopped
- 4 tsp. ground cumin
- 4 garlic cloves, minced
- 16 ounces dried black beans
- 7 cups hot water
- 1 tbsp. chopped chipotle chilies
- 2 tsp. coarse kosher salt
- 2 tsp. fresh lime juice
- 1/4 tsp. ground black pepper
- Optional toppings: sour cream and avocado

Directions

1. In a large skillet set over medium high heat, heat olive oil until hot but not smoky; sauté bell peppers and onion for about 8 minutes or until brown.
2. Stir in cumin and garlic for about 1 minute;
3. Transfer the mixture to a slow cooker and add 7 cups water, chipotles and beans and cook, covered, on high for about 3 hours or until beans are tender.

4. Transfer about 4 cups of the mixture to a blender and blend until very smooth; return the puree to the slow cooker and stir in salt, lime juice and pepper until well combined.

5. Ladle the soup into serving bowls and top with sour cream and avocado.

Irish Stew

Yield: 6 Servings
Total Time: 4 Hours 25 Minutes
Prep Time: 25 Minutes
Cook Time: 4 Hours

Ingredients
· 1 ¼ kg lamb neck chops, cut in halves
· 1 kg potatoes, diced
· 3 red onions, chopped
· ½ cup flour
· 2 tbsp. tomato paste
· 2 carrots, sliced
· 3 cups boiling water
· 1 cup parsley
· 3 beef stock cubes, crumbled

Directions
1. In a plastic bag, combine flour, salt and pepper and shake until well mixed; add the lamb chops and shake to coat well.

2. Transfer the lamb chops to a plate and reserve the flour.

3. Place half each of carrots, potatoes and onions in a slow cooker and top with half of the lamb chops.

Repeat the layers with the remaining carrots, potatoes, onions and chops.

4. In a small bowl, whisk the reserved flour with 2 tablespoons of cold water and tomato paste until well blended;

5. Gradually whisk in boiling water and stir in the stock cubes; pour the paste over the lamb chops and cook, covered, on low until the meat is tender and the sauce is thick.

6. Sprinkle with mint to serve.

Lemon Chicken Stew

Yield: 4 Servings
Total Time: 5 Hours 10 Minutes
Prep Time: 10 Minutes
Cook Time: 5 Hours

Ingredients
- 2 carrots, chopped
- 2 ribs celery, chopped
- 1 onion, chopped
- 20 large green olives
- 4 cloves garlic, crushed
- 2 bay leaves
- ½ tsp. dried oregano
- ¼ tsp. salt
- ¼ tsp. pepper
- 12 boneless skinless chicken thighs
- ¾ cup chicken stock
- ¼ cup almond flour
- 2 tbsp. lemon juice
- ½ cup chopped fresh parsley
- grated zest of 1 lemon

Directions
1. In slow cooker, combine carrots, celery, onion, olives, garlic, bay leaves, oregano, salt and pepper.
2. Arrange chicken pieces on top of vegetables.
3. Add broth and ¾ cup water. Cover and cook on low for 5 hours or until juices run clear when chicken is pierced.

4. Discard bay leaves. In a small bowl, whisk together a cup of cooking liquid and flour until very smooth; whisk in lemon juice and pour the mixture into your slow cooker.

5. Cover and cook on high for about 15 minutes or until thickened.

6. In a small bowl, mix together lemon zest and chopped parsley; sprinkled over the chicken mixture and serve. Enjoy!

Beef Chuck Cabbage Stew

Yield: 4 Servings
Total Time: 9 Hours 10 Minutes
Prep Time: 10 Minutes
Cook Time: 9 Hours

Ingredients
- 1 packet frozen baby carrots
- 2 medium onions, roughly chopped
- 1 small cabbage cored, and cut into 8 wedges
- 8 garlic cloves, peeled and smashed
- 2 bay leaves
- 8 pieces of beef chuck with marrow
- salt and freshly ground pepper to taste
- 2 tins diced tomatoes, drained
- 1 cup chicken stock

Directions
1. Place the baby carrots and chopped onions into the bottom of the slow cooker.
2. Layer the cabbage wedges on top.
3. Add crushed garlic cloves and bay leaves.
4. Season the beef shanks with salt and pepper (by the way, feel free to be pretty heavy-handed with the S&P).
5. Add beef shanks on top of vegetables.
6. Pour in the diced tomatoes and broth before putting on the lid.
7. Set the slow cooker on low for 9 hours.

Curried Chicken Stew

Yield: 8 Servings
Total Time: 4 Hours 20 Minutes
Prep Time: 20 Minutes
Cook Time: 4 Hours

Ingredients
· 8 bone-in chicken thighs
· 2 tbsp. olive oil or coconut oil
· 6 carrots, cut in 2-inch pieces
· 1 sweet onion, cut in thin wedges
· 1 cup unsweetened coconut milk
· 1/4 cup mild (or hot) curry paste
· Toasted almonds, coriander and fresh green or red chili (optional)

Directions
1. Cook chicken in a pan skin side down, in hot olive oil for 8 minutes, or until browned.
2. Remove from heat; drain and discard fat.
3. In a slow cooker combine carrots and onion.
4. In a bowl, combine curry paste and half of coconut milk; whisk until well blended and pour over carrots and onion.
5. Place the chicken over vegetables and pour over olive oil from the pan; cook, covered, on high for about 4 hours.
6. Remove chicken from the slow cooker and skim off excess fat from the sauce in the cooker; stir in remaining the coconut milk and serve stew in bowls.

7. Top each serving with toasted almonds, coriander, fresh chili and a dollop of yoghurt or crème fraiche.

Oxtail Stew

Yield: 4 Servings
Total Time: 9 Hours 10 Minutes
Prep Time: 10 Minutes
Cook Time: 9 Hours

Ingredients
· 1 ½ pounds oxtail
· 1 cup grated cabbage
· 1 cup grated carrots
· 2 large red onions, chopped
· 1 large bunch celery, chopped
· 1 cup diced tomatoes
· 2 jelly stock cubes
· 8 cups water
· 1 tbsp. crushed garlic
· 1 branch rosemary
· 2 bay leaves
· Grated cheese to serve

Directions
1. Place all ingredients into a slow cooker and cook on medium for 9 hours.
2. Season with salt and pepper
3. Sprinkle with grated cheese and serve.

Lamb & Cabbage Stew

Yield: 4 Servings
Total Time: 7 Hours 15 Minutes
Prep Time: 15 Minutes
Cook Time: 7 Hours

Ingredients

- 2 tbsp. coconut oil
- 500 g lamb chops, bone in
- 1 lamb or beef stock cube
- 2 cups water
- 1 cabbage, shredded
- 1 onion, sliced
- 2 carrots, chopped
- 2 sticks celery, chopped
- 1 tsp. dried thyme
- 1 tbsp. balsamic vinegar
- 1 tbsp. almond flour

Directions

1. Set the slow cooker to low then heat oil in a large frying pan and brown the lamb chops.
2. Add lamb to the slow cooker with remaining ingredients and mix until all ingredients are evenly distributed. Cook on low for 6-7 hours.
3. Remove bones from lamb.
4. For thicker a sauce, during the last 30 minutes of cooking, whisk about ¼ cup of the sauce with almond flour in a small bowl until combined; return the mixture to the slow cooker and stir well. Continue cooking for 30 minutes.

5. Serve and enjoy.

Rosemary-Garlic Beef Stew

Yield: 4 Servings
Total Time: 8 Hours 15 Minutes
Prep Time: 15 Minutes
Cook Time: 8 Hours

Ingredients
- 4 sticks celery, chopped
- 1 medium onion, sliced
- 2 tbsp. olive oil
- 4 medium carrots, diced
- 4 cloves garlic, minced
- 750g beef chuck
- Salt and pepper
- ¼ cup almond flour
- 2 cups beef stock
- 1 tbsp. Worcestershire sauce
- 2 tbsp. Dijon mustard
- 1 tbsp. soy sauce
- 1 tbsp. sugar
- ½ tbsp. dried rosemary
- ½ tsp. thyme

Directions
1. In a slow cooker, combine onion, carrots, and celery.

2. In a large bowl, combine stewing meat, almond flour, salt and pepper; work the meat with hands until well coated with the mixture.

3. In a nonstick pan, sauté garlic in hot oil until fragrant; add the meat and all the flour mixture; cook for about 4 minutes without stirring until brown.

4. Transfer the meat to a slow cooker and stir until well combined with the veggies.

5. Add in soy sauce, Worcestershire sauce, mustard, beef stock, thyme, rosemary and sugar to the skillet and cook, stirring, everything is well combined

6. Pour the sauce over the beef in the slow cooker and cover. Cook on low for about 8 hours. Stir and adjust the seasoning and then serve.

Beef Stew

Yield: 4 Servings
Total Time: 10 Hours 15 Minutes
Prep Time: 15 Minutes
Cook Time: 10 Hours

Ingredients
- 500g beef stewing meat, cubed
- 1 tsp. Salt
- 1 tsp. pepper
- 1 medium onion, finely chopped
- 2 celery ribs, sliced
- 2 cloves of garlic, minced
- 1 can tomato paste
- 3 cups beef stock
- 2 tbsp. Worcestershire sauce
- 2 cups frozen mixed veggies
- 1/4 cup almond flour
- 1/4 cup water

Directions
1. In a slow cooker, combine beef, tomato paste, beef broth, Worcestershire sauce, garlic, oregano, parsley, red onion, carrots, celery, salt and pepper; cook on low heat for about 10 hours.
2. During the last 30 minutes or cooking, mix water and flour in a small bowl and pour into the slow cooker.
3. Stir until well combined and then stir frozen veggies; cook for about 30 minutes and then serve.

Beef & Broccoli Stew

Yield: 4 Servings
Total Time: 2 Hours 50 Minutes
Prep Time: 20 Minutes
Cook Time: 2 Hours 30 Minutes

Ingredients
· 500g beef chuck roast, boneless, thinly sliced
· 1 cup beef stock
· 1/4 cup soy sauce
· 1/4 cup oyster sauce
· 1/4 cup sugar
· 2 tbsp. almond flour
· 3 cloves garlic, minced
· 1 tbsp. sesame oil
· 1 head broccoli, cut into florets

Directions
1. In a medium bowl, whisk together garlic, sesame oil, oyster sauce, soy sauce, sugar, and beef stock until well combined.
2. Place the beef in a slow cooker; stir in the sauce until well combined.
3. Cook, covered, on low for about 1 hour 30 minutes.
4. In a small bowl, whisk together almond flour and about 1/4 cup water; stir the mixture along with broccoli into the slow cooker.
5. Cook, covered, on low heat for an additional 1 hour.

Chicken Curry

Yields: 6 servings
Total Time: 8 Hours 10 Minutes
Prep Time: 10 Minutes
Cook Time: 8 Hours

Ingredients
- 2 pounds chicken breasts, boneless, skinless, diced
- 2 cups frozen peas
- 1 small onion, chopped (about one cup)
- 13.5oz can coconut milk
- 2 large cloves garlic, minced
- 3 tbsp. raw honey
- 6oz can tomato paste
- 14.5-oz can tomato sauce
- 1 tsp. crushed red pepper
- 2 tbsp. curry powder
- 1 tsp. sea salt

Directions
1. In a small bowl, mix garlic, tomato sauce, raw honey and seasoning; set aside.
2. Combine the remaining ingredients in a slow cooker; cover with the sauce mixture and cook on low for about 8 hours.
3. Serve with brown rice or pita bread.

Chicken & Chickpea Curry

Yield: 6 Servings
Total Time: 6 Hours 10 Minutes
Prep Time: 10 Minutes
Cook Time: 6 Hours

Ingredients
- 1 kg chicken thighs, quartered
- 1 tbsp. extra virgin olive oil
- 2 garlic cloves, crushed
- 1 red onion, chopped
- 1 cm piece ginger, grated
- 400g canned tomatoes
- ¼ curry paste
- ¼ cup chicken stock
- 400g canned chickpeas, rinsed
- 1/3 cup roasted cashew nuts, chopped
- ½ cup plain yogurt
- Lime wedges
- ¼ cup coriander leaves
- Cooked brown rice to serve

Directions
1. Heat oil in a large saucepan set over medium high heat; add chicken and cook, stirring, for about 5 minutes or until browned; transfer to a bowl.
2. Sauté garlic, onion and ginger in the same pan for about 4 minutes or until tender; stir in curry and cook for about 1 minute.
3. Return the chicken to the saucepan and stir in stock and tomatoes.

4. Transfer the mixture to a slow cooker and cook, covered, on low for about 6 hours or until chicken is tender.
5. Stir in chickpeas, nuts and yogurt and continue cooking for about 15 minutes.
6. Serve curry over rice, garnished with lime wedges and coriander.

Madras Lamb Curry

Yield: 4 Servings
Total Time: 5 Hours 15 Minutes
Prep Time: 15 Minutes
Cook Time: 5 Hours

Ingredients
· 8 fatty lamb chops
· 6 tbsp. coconut milk
· 2 cups water
· 3 tbsp. red curry paste
· 2 tbsp. Thai fish sauce
· 1 tbsp. dried onion flakes
· 2 tbsp. dried Thai or fresh red chilies
· 1 tbsp. brown sugar
· 1 tbsp. ground cumin
· 1 tbsp. ground coriander
· 1/8 tsp, ground cloves
· 1/8 tsp. ground nutmeg
· 1 tbsp. ground ginger

To Serve
· 2 tbsp. coconut milk powder
· 1 tbsp. red curry paste
· 2 tbsp. brown sugar
· 1/4 cup cashews, roughly chopped
· 1/4 cup fresh cilantro, chopped

Directions
1. Place the raw lamb chops in a large slow cooker. Add the 6 tbsp. coconut milk, water, red curry paste, fish

sauce, onion flakes, chilies, brown sugar cumin, coriander, cloves, nutmeg, and ginger.

2. Cover and cook on high for about 5 hours (or low for 8).

3. Just before serving, scoop out the meat to another dish. Then whisk into the sauce the coconut milk powder, curry paste, sugar.

4. Break the meat into pieces and stir into the sauce, along with the chopped cashews.

5. Garnish with chopped coriander before serving.

Spinach & Lamb Curry

Yield: 4 Servings
Total Time: 8 Hours 25 Minutes
Prep Time: 25 Minutes
Cook Time: 8 Hours

Ingredients
· 1/3 cup coconut oil
· 3 yellow onions , chopped
· 4 cloves garlic , minced
· 1 tbsp. grated ginger
· 2 tsp. ground cumin
· 1 1/2 tsp. cayenne pepper
· 1 1/2 tsp. ground turmeric
· 2 cups beef stock , preferably high quality
· 900g leg of lamb , cut into 2cm cubes
    · Salt
· 6 cups baby spinach
· 1 1/2 cups plain full-fat yogurt

Directions
1. In a large pan set over medium high heat, heat oil for about 5 minutes or until golden brown. Stir in turmeric, cayenne, cumin, and ginger and sauté for about 30 seconds or until fragrant.
2. Pour in broth scraping up the browned bits on the bottom. When broth comes to a boil, remove pan from heat.

3. Put lamb in the slow cooker, and sprinkle with 1 tbsp. salt. Add contents of frying pan. Cover and cook on low for 8 hours.
4. Add baby spinach to pot and cook, stirring occasionally, until spinach is wilted, about 5 minutes.
5. Let it cool off completely before storing in the freezer.
6. When you are ready to eat, after thawing the stew, stir in the yogurt as it heats up before serving.

Chicken & Turkey

Thai Turkey Legs

Yield: 2 Servings
Total Time: 4 Hours 7 Minutes
Prep Time: 7 Minutes
Cook Time: 4 Hours

Ingredients
· 1 ½ pounds turkey legs
· 2 cups coconut milk
· 1 tbsp. lime juice
· 1½ tsp. lemon garlic seasoning
· Lime wedges
· ¼ cup fresh cilantro
· 1 tsp. ghee

Directions

1. In a skillet set over medium heat, melt the ghee and sauté the turkey until browned
2. Add coconut milk into the slow cooker and stir in lime juice, lime wedge, lemon garlic seasoning and cilantro.
3. Add the turkey legs and cook on high for about 3 hours.

Herbed Turkey Breast

Yield: 6 Servings
Total Time: 4 Hours 10 Minutes
Prep Time: 10 Minutes
Cook Time: 4 Hours

Ingredients
- 3 pounds turkey breast (bone-in)
- ¼ cup whipped cream cheese, spread with garden veggies
- 2 tbsp. softened butter
- 1 tbsp. soy sauce
- ½ tsp. dried basil
- 1 tbsp. minced parsley
- ½ tsp. dried thyme
- ½ tsp. dried sage
- ¼ tsp. garlic powder
- ¼ tsp sea salt
- ¼ tsp. ground black pepper

Directions
1. In a small bowl, combine the ingredients until well blended; brush the mixture over the turkey breast and place in a slow cooker.
2. Cover and cook on low for about 4 hours or until turkey is tender.

Tangy Turkey Meatballs

Yield: 32 Meatballs
Total Time: 2 Hours 30 Minutes
Prep Time: 30 Minutes
Cook Time: 2 Hours

Ingredients

For meatballs

· 1 ½ pounds ground turkey
· ½ cup panko breadcrumbs
· ½ tsp. onion powder
· ½ tsp. garlic salt
· ½ tsp. chili powder
· 1 egg

For sauce

· 2 ½ tbsp. raw honey
· 1 cup tomato sauce
· 2 tbsp. white vinegar
· 2 tbsp. Worcestershire sauce
· ½ tsp. onion powder
· ½ tsp. chili powder
· ½ tsp. garlic salt

Directions

1. Preheat oven to 350°F.
2. In a large bowl, mix ground turkey, breadcrumbs, onion powder, garlic salt, chili powder, and egg until well combined; roll the mixture into 1-inch balls and arrange them on a greased baking sheet.

3. Bake for about 20 minutes; remove the meatballs from oven and set aside to cool.
4. In a slow cooker, combine all sauce ingredients until well combined; add the meatballs and stir until covered.
5. Cook on low for about 2 hours.

Turkey Breast

Yield: 12 Servings
Total Time: 8 Hours 10 Minutes
Prep Time: 10 Minutes
Cook Time: 8 Hours

Ingredients
- 6 pounds of turkey breast
- 1 ounce dry onion soup mix

Directions
1. Rub the soup mix under and outside the skin and place it in a slow cooker.
2. Cook, covered, on high for about 1 hour and then set heat to low. Cook for about 7 more hours.

Ginger Peach Chicken

Yield: 3 Servings
Total Time: 5 Hours 10 Minutes
Prep Time: 10 Minutes
Cook Time: 5 Hours

Ingredients
· 1 pound chicken thighs, boneless, skinless
· 3 cloves garlic, minced
· 1-inch fresh ginger root, grated
· 1 tbsp. low-sodium soy sauce
· 1 cup peach jam

Directions
1. Place the chicken thighs in the slow cooker.
2. In a small bowl, mix ginger, garlic, peach jam, and soy sauce until well blended; spoon the sauce over the chicken and cover the pot with lid.
3. Cook on low for about 5 hours or until chicken is cooked through and shreds easily.
4. Remove the chicken from the cooker and shred.
5. Return and let sit for a few minutes to mix with juice.
6. Serve with cooked brown rice.

Asian Chicken

Yields: 6 servings
Total Time: 5 Hours 5 Minutes
Prep Time: 5 Minutes
Cook Time: 5 Hours

Ingredients
· 2 pounds of ground chicken
· 4 cloves garlic, minced
· 2 large carrots, grated
· 1 medium red bell pepper, diced
· 1 tbsp. raw honey
· 1/4 cup low-sodium soy sauce
· 1/4 tsp. crushed red pepper flakes
· 1/4 cup ketchup

Directions
1. Combine all ingredients in your crockpot and cook on low heat for about 5 hours or until chicken is tender.
2. Shred the chicken and serve.

Meat Recipes

Healthy Doner Kebabs

Yield: 4 Servings

Total Time: 4 Hours 10 Minutes

Prep Time: 10 Minutes

Cook Time: 4 Hours

Ingredients

· 500g lamb mince

· 1 tsp. mixed herbs

· 1 tsp. oregano

· 1 ½ tsp. garlic powder

· 1 ½ tsp. cayenne pepper

· 1 tsp. pepper

· 1 tsp salt

· Lettuce and cucumber to serve

· Pitas

Directions

1. In a bowl, mix all the ingredients, except mince, until well combined; mix in mince and roll into a loaf shape.

2. Place the loaf in a slow cooker and cook on low for about 6 hours; remove from heat and wrap in tin foil; let it rest for at least 10 minutes.

3. Meanwhile, warm the pitas and prepare salad.

4. Thinly slice the kebab; fill the pitas with sliced kebab, lettuce and cucumber. Enjoy!

Short Ribs

Yield: 4 Servings
Total Time: 10 Hours 30 Minutes
Prep Time: 30 Minutes
Cook Time: 10 Hours

Ingredients
· 2.7kg beef short ribs (English style)
· ½ cup coconut aminos
· 6 cloves garlic, peeled
· 1 cup homemade bone broth or a low sodium variety
· 1 Asian pear, peeled, cored and chopped
· ¼ cup freshly minced cilantro
· 3 spring onions, chopped
· 1 inch ginger root, peeled and sliced
· 1 tbsp apple cider vinegar
· 2 tsp fish sauce
· Freshly ground pepper and kosher salt to taste

Directions
1. Place an oven rack about 5 inches from your oven's heating element and preheat your broiler.
2. Liberally season your short ribs with salt and pepper. Line a baking sheet with kitchen foil and arrange the ribs on a single layer with the bone side facing up. Broil for 5 minutes on each side until evenly browned.
3. Transfer the ribs to your slow-cooker, arranging them on a single layer.
4. Combine all the remaining ingredients apart from the cilantro in your blender and pulse until puréed.

Pour the sauce over the ribs, cover the pot and coo for 8-10 hours on low.

5. Once you are ready to eat, ladle the excess fat from the surface and garnish with cilantro before serving

Mocha Rubbed Pot Roast

Yield: 6 servings
Total Time: 6 Hours 20 Minutes
Prep Time: 20 Minutes
Cook Time: 6 Hours

Ingredients

For the pot roast:
- 2 pounds grass fed chuck
- 1 cup beef broth
- 1 cup brewed coffee
- 7 dried figs, chopped
- ½ onion, chopped
- 3 tablespoons balsamic vinegar

For the rub:
- 2 tablespoons smoked paprika
- 2 tablespoons finely ground coffee beans
- 1 tablespoon freshly ground black pepper
- 1 teaspoon sweet paprika
- 1 tablespoon cacao powder
- 1 teaspoon, ground ginger
- 1 teaspoon red chili powder
- 1 teaspoon kosher salt

Directions

1. Combine all the rub ingredients in a small bowl and mix well to combine. (Store the extra in an airtight container)
2. Use a paper towel to pat the chuck dry then generously rub the mocha rub on all sides of the roast using your hands.
3. Mix the beef broth, coffee, figs, onions and balsamic vinegar in a power blender and process until smooth and pour into your slow cooker. Add the roast and cook for 6 hours.
4. Shred the roast using two folks and boil down the sauce until thick and pour over the shredded roast.

Lamb-Bacon Chowder

Yield: 4 Servings
Total Time: 6-8 Hours
Prep Time: 20 Minutes
Cook Time: 6-8 Hours
Ingredients
· 4 cloves garlic, minced
· 1 leek, sliced
· 2 celery ribs, diced
· 200g button mushrooms, sliced
· 2 Vidalia onions, thinly sliced
· 4 tbsp. butter
· 2 cups chicken stock
· 500g lamb, cut in cubes
· 8 oz. cream cheese

- 1 cup heavy cream
- 1 packet streaky bacon – cooked crisp, and crumbled
- 1 tsp. salt
- 1 tsp. pepper
- 1 tsp. garlic powder
- 1 tsp. thyme

Directions

1. Heat your slow cooker on low setting and add the garlic, leeks, celery, mushrooms, onions, 2 tbsp. butter, 1 cup chicken stock, and salt and pepper.
2. Cover, and cook vegetables on low for 1 hour.
3. Pan-sear the lamb in the remaining butter until they are browned on both sides.
4. Add the remaining 1 cup of chicken stock. Using a spatula scrape up any bits of lamb that may be stuck to the pan.
5. Add chicken stock to slow cooker. Add heavy cream, cream cheese, garlic powder, and thyme to slow cooker. Stir well until there are no longer chunks of cream cheese visible.
6. Add the lamb to the slow cooker, along with bacon. Stir until all ingredients are well combined. Cover and cook for 6-8 hours.

Lemon Infused Lamb Stew

Yield: 4 Servings
Total Time: 6 Hours 15 Minutes
Prep Time: 15 Minutes
Cook Time: 6 Hours

Ingredients
· 2 carrots, chopped
· 2 celery ribs, chopped
· 1 onion, chopped
· 20 large green olives
· 4 cloves garlic, crushed
· 2 bay leaves
· ½ tsp. dried oregano
· ¼ tsp. salt
· ¼ tsp. pepper
· 500g lamb, cut in large cubes
· ¾ cup chicken stock
· ¼ cup almond
· 2 tbsp. lemon juice
· ½ cup chopped fresh parsley
· grated zest of 1 lemon

Directions
1. In your slow cooker, combine carrots, celery, onion, olives, garlic, bay leaves, oregano, salt and pepper.
2. Arrange the lamb pieces on top of the vegetables. Add broth and ¾ cup water.
3. Cover and cook on low for 5-1/2 to 6 hours or until cooked to desire.

4. In a small bowl, mix 1 cup of cooking liquid and flour; whisk until very smooth and then whisk in lemon juice. Pour this mixture into your slow cooker; cook, covered, on high heat for about 15 minutes or until thickened and then turn off the cooker.
5. Allow to cool completely before packing the food in freezer friendly bags or jars.
6. When ready to serve, garnish with parsley and zest after heating.

Beef Chuck & Green Cabbage Stew

Yield: 4-6 Servings
Total Time: 9 Hours 20 Minutes
Prep Time: 20 Minutes
Cook Time: 9Hours

Ingredients
· 1 packet frozen baby carrots
· 2 onions, roughly chopped
· 1 small cabbage cored, and cut into 8 wedges
· 8 garlic cloves, smashed
· 2 bay leaves
· 8 pieces of beef chuck with marrow
· salt and freshly ground pepper to taste
· 2 tins diced tomatoes, drained
· 1 cup chicken stock

Directions
1. Place baby carrots and chopped onions into the bottom of the slow cooker. Layer the cabbage wedges on top and add the crushed garlic cloves and bay leaves
2. Season the beef shanks generously with salt and pepper then add them on top of the veggies.
3. Pour in the diced tomatoes and broth before putting on the lid. Set the slow cooker on low and cook for 9 hours.

Hearty Beef Stew

Yield: 4 Servings
Total Time: 8 Hours 15 Minutes
Prep Time: 15 Minutes
Cook Time: 8 Hours

Ingredients

- 600g stewing beef (fatty cuts of meat will yield better results)
- 3 tbsp. olive oil
- 2 cups beef stock
- 1 packet streaky bacon, cooked crisp and crumbled
- 2 cans diced tomatoes, drained
- 1 cup mixed bell peppers, chopped
- 1 cup mushrooms ,quartered
- 2 celery ribs, chopped
- 1 carrot, chopped
- 1 onion, chopped
- 2 large cloves garlic, minced
- 2 tbsp. organic tomato paste
- 2 tbsp. Worcestershire sauce
- 1 tsp. sea salt
- 1 ½ tsp. black pepper
- 1 tsp. garlic powder
- 1 tsp. onion powder
- 1 tsp. dried oregano

Directions

1. In a large pan over medium-high heat, sear the beef in olive oil, browning on both sides then transfer to slow cooker.
2. Stir in mushrooms, bell peppers, tomatoes, bacon, tomato paste, garlic, onion, carrot, celery, dried oregano, onion powder, garlic powder, Worcestershire sauce, sea salt and black pepper.
3. Cover and cook on low 8 hours.

Curried Goat Stew

Yield: 4 Servings
Total Time: 7-8 Hours
Prep Time: 15 Minutes
Cook Time: 7-8 Hours

Ingredients

· 8 goat chops
· 2 tbsp. olive oil or coconut oil
· 6 carrots, cut in 2-inch pieces
· 1 sweet onion, cut in thin wedges
· 1 cup unsweetened coconut milk
· 1/4 cup mild (or hot) curry paste
· Toasted almonds, coriander and fresh green or red chili

Directions

1. Cook the chops in a pan in hot oil for 8 minutes, or until browned. Remove from heat; drain and discard fat.
2. In a slow cooker combine carrots and onion. Whisk together half the coconut milk and the curry paste then pour over carrots and onion.
3. Place the goat meat on top of vegetables and pour over oil from pan.
4. Cover and cook on low for 7 to 8 hours.
5. Remove chops from slow cooker. Remove the excess fat from sauce in cooker; add the remaining coconut milk and stir to mix well.

6. When serving, top with chopped toasted almonds and a dollop of plain Greek yogurt.

Tomato Bredie

Yield: 4 Servings
Total Time: 7 Hours 15 Minutes
Prep Time: 15 Minutes
Cook Time: 7 Hours

Ingredients
- 1 tbsp. olive oil
- 8 mutton chops
- 2 tbsp. almond flour
- 1 large onion, chopped
- 8 fresh tomatoes, finely chopped
- 1 tsp. salt
- 1/2 tsp. freshly ground black pepper
- 2 bay leaves
- 1 tsp. Xylitol
- 1 tbsp. white vinegar
- 1 dash Worcestershire sauce
- 1 cube lamb stock

Directions

1. Heat oil over medium-high heat in a large, heavy-bottomed saucepan.
2. Dredge the meat in almond flour and cook in hot oil until well browned. Stir in onions, and cook for about 5 minutes or until soft.
3. Transfer this to your slow cooker and mix in the tomatoes. Season with salt, black pepper, white peppercorns, bay leaves, xylitol, vinegar, Worcestershire sauce, and lamb bouillon.

4. Cover, and cook on low for 7 hours.

Balsamic Pork

Yield: 4 Servings
Total Time: 8 Hours 25 Minutes
Prep Time: 25 Minutes
Cook Time: 8 Hours

Ingredients
- 450g pork roast
- 1/2 cup balsamic vinegar
- 1/3 cup honey
- 2 tsp. fresh rosemary
- 1/2 tsp. dried thyme
- 2 bay leaves
- 2 tsp. salt
- 1/4 tsp. black pepper

Directions
1. Place pork roast in your slow cooker. Mix all ingredients in a bowl and pour over the roast.
2. Cook on low for 8 hours.
3. Remove the cooked roast from the slow-cooker. Cover and let cool.
4. Transfer the remaining sauce from pot to a saucepan; bring to a boil and cook until reduced by half.
5. Freeze the roast by wrapping it tightly in aluminum foil before putting it in a freezer friendly bag. Pack the sauce in a separate freezer bag and freeze them until you are ready to eat.

6. When ready, slice the roast after heating it up and drizzle the sauce on top before serving.

Vegetarian Recipes

Cinnamon Bread Casserole

Yield: 6 Servings
Total Time: 12 Hours
Prep Time: 4 Hours
Cook Time: 8 Hours

Ingredients
· 1 loaf of cinnamon bread, cut in cubes
· 3 ½ cups almond milk
· 3 eggs
· 1 tbsp. bourbon vanilla extract
· 1 tsp. cinnamon
· ½ tsp. nutmeg
· 75g sugar
· 1 pinch sea salt
· For the nut streusel:
· ½ cup toasted pecans, chopped
· 2 tbsp. brown sugar
· 2 tbsp. all-purpose flour
· 2 tbsp. butter

Directions
1. Combine all the bread casserole ingredients apart from the bread cubes in a mixing bowl until well mixed.
2. Add the bread cubes to a large bowl and add the wet ingredients on top. Toss well to combine, cover with cling wrap and chill in your fridge for 4 hours.

3. Generously grease your slow cooker and turn the heat to low. Add the bread casserole mix and cook for 8 hours.

4. When remaining with half an hour of cook time, mix the nutty streusel ingredients and sprinkle over the bread casserole and continue cooking.

5. Allow to cool completely then wrap tightly in aluminum foil and arrange in a freezing jar then place in your freezer.

Mushroom Stroganoff

Yield: 4 Servings
Total Time: 4 hours 30 Minutes
Prep Time: 15 Minutes
Cook Time: 4 Hours 15 Minutes

Ingredients

For the stroganoff:
- 500g shiitake mushrooms, sliced
- 3cloves garlic, finely sliced
- 2 Vidalia onions, diced
- 1 bouillon cube, dissolved in 600ml hot water
- 1 tbsp. butter
- 2 tbsp. tomato ketchup
- 5 tbsp. sour cream
- 3 tsp. sweet paprika
- 3 tbsp. fresh parsley, chopped and some for garnish

For the spaghetti (to be prepared when ready to serve – not to be frozen):
- 1 pk spaghetti
- 3 cloves garlic, crushed
- 3tbsp olive oil
- Grated parmesan cheese
- Red pepper flakes, to taste
- Freshly ground black pepper, to taste
- Kosher salt to taste

Directions

1. In a skillet over medium heat, heat the butter and sauté the mushrooms and onions for about 5-10

minutes until soft but not browned. Remove from heat and transfer to your slow cooker. Add in the paprika, garlic, bouillon water and ketchup.

2. Turn the cooker's heat setting to high and cook for 4 hours.

3. Turn off your slow cooker and stir in the parsley and sour cream. If you want a thicker sauce, transfer the stroganoff to a saucepan and simmer on low heat for 15 minutes. Turn off the heat and set aside to cool completely.

4. Once cool, transfer the stroganoff to a freezer friendly jar or freezer bags and freeze for up to 6 months.

For the spaghetti:

1. Cook thee spaghetti according to package instructions then drain, reserving a cup of the cooking fluid.

2. Place a saucepan over medium heat and add the oil. Sauté the garlic then stir in the black pepper, pepper flakes and salt and cook for half a minute, stirring all along.

3. Pour in the spaghetti and toss well until evenly coated. Pour in half of the reserved fluid and cook for one minute then remove from heat.

Minestrone

Yield: 4 Servings
Total Time: 8 hours 20 Minutes
Prep Time: 20 Minutes
Cook Time: 8 Hours

Ingredients
- 400g crushed tomatoes
- 100g white kidney beans
- 100g red kidney beans
- ½ cup green beans
- 2 cups fresh spinach, chopped
- 1 medium onion, chopped
- 3 cloves garlic, crushed
- 1 celery stalk, diced
- ½ zucchini, diced
- 1 carrot, diced
- 3 cups veggie stock
- ¼ cup parmesan, finely grated
- 1 tsp oregano
- ½ tbsp fresh parsley, minced
- 1/2 tsp dried thyme
- 1 pinch freshly ground black pepper
- ¼ cup elbow macaroni
- Salt to taste

For the garlic bread – to be served when ready to eat:
- 1 loaf crusty bread, split into 4
- 2 tbsp. butter
- 4 garlic cloves, minced

· 3 tbsp. grated parmesan

Directions

1. Mix all the minestrone ingredients apart from the spinach and cheese in your slow cooker then turn it to low. Cook for 8 hours.

2. When you have 30 minutes of cook time to go, boil some salted water in a saucepan and stir in the macaroni once the water starts boiling. Cook aldante then pour these into your slow cooker together with the spinach. Cook for 15 minutes then top with parmesan. Turn off your slow cooker.

3. Let the minestrone cool completely then pack it in freezer bags or jars.

For the garlic bread:

1. Once you have thawed the minestrone and it's heating up; combine olive oil, garlic and butter in a small dish and microwave for a minute or you can combine in a small pan over low heat for 3 minutes.

2. Toast the bread in your broiler until golden brown and generously brush it with the garlic mixture. Sprinkle with the cheese and broil for a further 30 seconds. Cut up the bread into large chunks and serve with the hot minestrone.

Asian Saag Aloo

Yield: 4-6 Servings
Total Time: 4 hours 10 Minutes
Prep Time: 10 Minutes
Cook Time: 4Hours

Ingredients
- 500g fresh spinach, roughly chopped
- 200g fresh baby spinach
- 2 tbsp. ginger root, crushed
- 4 cloves garlic, crushed
- 350ml coconut milk
- ¼ cup frozen peas
- 2 pkts marinated tofu
- 1 cup tomato sauce
- 2 tbsp. tomato ketchup
- 1 tbsp. ground coriander
- 1 tbsp. ground cumin
- 1 tbsp. garam masala
- 1 pinch cayenne pepper
- 2 tbsp. cilantro, chopped
- Salt to taste

Directions
1. First, set aside the baby spinach, tofu and frozen peas. Combine all the remaining ingredients in your slow cooker. Set it to low and cook for 4 hours.
2. Use an immersion blender to puree the entire mixture after 3 hours 35 minutes of cooking (You can omit the blending part if you don't like your food

mushy). Fold in the baby spinach, peas and the tofu, cover the slow cooker and cook for the remaining minutes.

3. Allow to cool completely before packing the sag aloo in freezer friendly bags or jars.

4. When ready to eat, thaw and heat and serve with roast potatoes.

Three Bean Pilaf

Yield: 4-6 Servings
Total Time: 2 hours 40 Minutes
Prep Time: 10 Minutes
Cook Time: 2 Hours 30 Minutes

Ingredients
· 200g canned black-eyed peas, do not drain
· 100g canned navy beans, do not drain
· 100g canned white kidney beans, do not drain
· 750g diced tomato with the juices
· 280g canned sweet corn, do not drain
· 2 cups cooked rice
· 1 purple onion, chopped
· 1 green pepper, diced
· 3 cloves garlic, finely chopped
· ½ cup cheddar cheese, shredded
· ¼ cup mild chili powder
· 1/2 tbsp. ground cumin

Directions
1. Mix the peas, beans, tomatoes, corn, onion, pepper, garlic, cumin and chili powder in a slow cooker. Stir well to combine and turn it on high and cook for 2 hours.
2. After the 2 hours, stir in 2 cups of the cooked rice together with the cheese and cool for 30 more minutes. Turn off the slow cooker and allow the pilaf to cool completely.

3. Pack tightly in aluminum foil then place in a freezer friendly jar and put it in your freezer.

Spicy Veggie Chili

Yield: 5 Servings
Total Time: 5 hours 25 Minutes
Prep Time: 25 Minutes
Cook Time: 5 Hours

Ingredients

- 150g canned black beans, rinsed
- 150g canned kidney beans, rinsed
- 150g canned garbanzo beans, rinsed
- 1/3 cup canned corn, drained
- 2 tbsp. tomato sauce
- 3 tbsp. tomato paste
- 1 tbsp. olive oil
- 1 green pepper, yellow pepper and red pepper, chopped
- 2 cloves garlic, minced
- 1 onion, chopped
- 200 g spinach, chopped
- ¼ yellow squash, chopped
- 1 small zucchini, chopped
- 1 cup vegetable stock
- 2 tbsp. chili powder
- 1tbsp oregano
- 1tbsp ground cumin
- 1tbsp dried parsley
- A good pinch freshly ground black pepper

Directions

1. In a large pan, heat the olive oil over medium heat and cook the onions, garlic and the peppers for 10 minutes. Turn off the heat and transfer this mixture into your slow cooker. Stir in the rest of the ingredients and cook on low for 5 hours then turn off your slow cooker.
2. Freeze the chili in freezer friendly bags or jars.
3. When you are ready to eat, thaw the chili then heat over medium heat, add some shredded cheddar cheese and continue heating until melted. Serve with corn chips.

Veggie Sloppy Joes

Yield: 5 Servings
Total Time: 5 hours 30 Minutes

Prep Time: 30 Minutes
Cook Time: 5 Hours

Ingredients
- ½ cup dry pinto beans, soaked overnight
- ½ cup corn
- 2 cups green cabbage, thinly shredded
- 1 carrot, sliced
- 1 small zucchini, chopped
- 2 cloves garlic, minced
- 1 onion, sliced
- 1 red pepper, diced
- 1 ½ tbsp. honey mustard
- 1 tbsp. balsamic vinegar
- 1 tbsp. extra virgin olive oil
- 1 tbsp. soy sauce, low sodium
- ¼ cup water
- 1 ½ tbsp. chili powder
- 1 tbsp. tomato paste
- 115 ml tomato sauce, unsalted
- ½ tbsp. brown sugar
- Salt to taste
- 5 whole wheat burger buns, for serving

Direction

1. Add the oil to a large skillet over medium heat. Stir in the onions and the carrots and cook for 8 minutes until they start browning. Stir in garlic and chili powder and cook until fragrant for 20 seconds. Turn off the heat and stir in the balsamic vinegar and scrape up any bits.

2. Generously coat your slow cooker with cooking spray and add the drained soaked beans. Gently stir in the tomato sauce and paste, soy sauce, water and bell pepper. Carefully spread the carrot mixture on top of the beans, careful not to stir them together so the beans to stay moist throughout the cooking process.

3. Turn your slow cooker to high and cook for 5 hours.

4. Now stir in the shredded cabbage, corn, zucchini, sugar, honey mustard and salt and let them cook for the remaining half hour.

Spicy Lentil Stew

Yield: 4 Servings
Total Time: 8 hours 45 Minutes
Prep Time: 15 Minutes
Cook Time: 8 Hours 30 Minutes

Ingredients
· 1 cup dry red lentils, rinsed
· 2 red onions, finely chopped
· 3 cloves garlic, minced
· 1 tbsp. ginger, peeled and minced
· 400g can chopped tomatoes
· 1 cup coconut milk
· 2 cups vegetable broth
· 1 tbsp. canola oil
· 1 tsp. cumin seed
· 1 tsp. ground coriander
· 1 tsp. freshly ground black pepper
· Salt and chili flakes to taste

Directions
1. Pour the oil into a skillet over medium heat. Sauté the onions for 3 minutes then stir in the ginger, garlic, cumin, coriander and black pepper. Keep stirring for a minute or so then stir in the tomatoes, lentils and stock.
2. Transfer to your slow cooker and cook on low for 8 hours.

3. Slowly add the coconut milk and season with salt and chili flakes. Cook for an additional 30 minutes then turn off the slow cooker.

4. Let the lentil stew cool completely before transferring it into freezer bags or jars.

Lentil-Navy Bean Stew

Yield: 4-6 Servings
Total Time: 8 -10 Hours
Prep Time: 10 Minutes
Cook Time: 8 – 10 Hours

Ingredients
- ½ cup dry navy beans
- ½ cup dry red lentils
- 5 small carrots, sliced
- 1 cup barley
- ½ cup red wine
- 900 ml vegetable juice
- 2 cups celery, sliced
- ¼ cup brown sugar
- 2 large onions, chopped
- 2 bay leaves
- 1 tsp. freshly ground black pepper
- ½ tsp. thyme
- A good pinch garlic powder
- Salt to taste
- 2 cups water

Directions
1. Combine all the ingredients in your slow cooker and cook on low for 8-10 hours. Discard the bay leaves once the stew is ready and turn of the cooker.
2. Allow the stew to cool completely then scoop it into freezer friendly bags or jars and place them in the freezer.

Sweet Potato Veggie Chili

Yield: 4 Servings
Total Time: 8 Hours 15 Minutes
Prep Time: 15 Minutes
Cook Time: 8 Hours

Ingredients
- 1 sweet potato, peeled and cut into cubes
- 2 ounces pumpkin, diced
- 400 g can fire roasted tomatoes, diced
- 1 red onion, chopped
- 4 cloves garlic, crushed
- 1 green pepper, chopped
- 250 g can kidney beans, rinsed and drained
- 250 g can black beans, rinsed and drained
- 2tsp cocoa powder, unsweetened
- 1 tbsp. chili powder
- ¼ tsp. cinnamon powder
- 1 tbsp. ground cumin
- Kosher salt and freshly ground black pepper to taste

Directions

1. Add the onions, garlic, green pepper, cocoa and the spices to your slow cooker and stir well to combine. Add the remaining chili ingredients, season with salt and pepper and add a cup of water. Cover and cook on low for 8 hours until the sweet potatoes are nice and soft.

2. Once the chili has cooled completely, freeze it in freezer friendly bags or jars.

3. When ready to eat the chili, thaw and heat it and garnish with sliced green onions, radishes and a dollop of sour cream.

Ratatouille

Yield: 4 Servings
Total Time: 9 Hours 15 Minutes
Prep Time: 15 Minutes
Cook Time: 9 Hours

Ingredients

- 1 egg plant, halved then sliced
- 1 green pepper, cut in strips (deseeded)
- 1 onion, halved then sliced
- 1 tomatoes, wedged
- 2 small zucchinis, sliced
- 75 ml tomato paste
- 1/8 cup olive oil
- 2tbsp fresh parsley
- 1tsp dried basil
- 1tsp sugar
- ½ tsp. oregano
- ½ tsp. freshly ground black pepper
- Salt and red pepper flakes to taste
- Grated parmesan for sprinkling

Directions

1. Layer the vegetables on your slow cooker by starting with onions, eggplant, zucchini, garlic, followed by the peppers and finally the tomatoes. Sprinkle with half the dried herbs, sugar, parsley, salt and the pepper flakes. Add half the tomato paste and repeat the layering in the same order.

2. Next, drizzle with the olive oil and turn your slow cooker to low and cook for 9 hours.

3. Once ready, allow to cool completely and pack tightly in aluminum foil before transferring to a freezer friendly tin.

Cauliflower 'Mashed Potatoes'

Yield: 4 Servings
Total Time: 6 Hours 10 Minutes
Prep Time: 10 Minutes
Cook Time: 6 Hours

Ingredients
· 1 whole cauliflower , cut into florets
· 4 cloves garlic, peeled and roughly chopped
· 1 tbsp. butter
· 2 tbsp. cream cheese
· 1 bay leaf
· Milk (optional)
· 3 cups water
· Salt and pepper to taste

Directions
1. Combine the cauliflower florets in your slow cooker with all the ingredients apart from the milk and cheese. Cover the cooker and turn it on low and cook for 5-6 hours.
2. Discard the bay leaf and garlic cloves and drain off the water. Mash the cauliflower using a potato masher or an immersion blender if you want it very creamy. If you are adding milk, do so a tablespoon at a time, until you get the desired consistency. Blend in the cream cheese.
3. Allow to cool completely then pack tightly in aluminum foil before wrapping it in a freezer friendly bag.

4. Once you are ready to serve, that and heat the mash then season with salt and pepper and garnish with chopped chives or chopped green onions and serve with your favorite stew. Enjoy!

Chicken Recipes

Chicken is one of the most versatile of all meats and also one of the cheapest. It lends itself well to freezer cooking because it freezes well, thaws quickly and takes to a number of different seasonings well.

Chicken Divan

Chicken Divan is an easy dish that is enjoyed by most. Add some brown rice on the side for a healthy, flavorful meal.

Serves 8
Method: Prepare recipe and freeze uncooked. Cook when ready to eat.
Ingredients:

- **3 large bunches of broccoli crowns, chopped into bite-size pieces**

- 4 c. cooked chicken
- 2 c. milk
- ½ c. cream
- 1 can (14 oz.) low-sodium chicken broth
- ½ c. butter
- ½ c. flour
- ¾ c. cheddar cheese, shredded
- ¼ c. parmesan cheese
- ½ tab. Worcestershire sauce
- ½ teas. pepper
- Salt to taste
- ½ c. bread crumbs

To prepare for the freezer: Steam broccoli until crisp-tender, drain and set aside.

In a large saucepan, melt butter over medium heat and stir in flour. Stirring constantly, cook about 2 minutes or until the mix is a light brown color. Slowly add in the milk, cream and chicken broth. Stir constantly. Cook about 5 minutes or until the mixture thickens.

Stir in ¼ cup cheddar cheese, the parmesan cheese, Worcestershire sauce, pepper and salt to taste. Stir over low heat until the cheese melts.

Place chicken and broccoli in two 9" x 9" pans, or one 13" x 9" pan. Pour sauce over, and then sprinkle with remaining cheese and bread crumbs. Cool and then freeze.

When you're ready to eat: Thaw for 24 hours or cook from frozen. If thawed, cook at 350 for 30 minutes or until heated through; if frozen, cook 45 minutes to 1 hour or until heated through.

Drunken Chicken

The chicken's not really drunk and this is safe for most to eat because the alcohol does cook out, but the beer adds a hearty flavor and adds a tenderness to the chicken that makes this just delectable. It also has a kick!

Serves 8 (2 bags of 4 servings each).
Method: Freeze in the marinade and cook when ready to eat.
Ingredients:
- **8 boneless skinless chicken breasts**
- 2 (12 oz.) bottles of beer
- ½ c. Dijon mustard
- ¼ c. + 2 tab. olive oil
- 4 cloves garlic, thinly sliced
- 2 tab. Worcestershire sauce
- 2 teas. kosher salt
- 1 teas. black pepper
- ½ teas. Tabasco sauce

To prepare for the freezer: Mix all ingredients except the chicken in a large bowl. Divide evenly among the two bags and add four chicken breasts to each bag. Freeze.

When you're ready to eat: Thaw the chicken in the refrigerator overnight. Remove the chicken from the marinade and discard the marinade. Dry the chicken well with paper towels and then grill on an outdoor grill until the chicken is cooked through. You can also cook these on a stovetop or countertop grill. A final option is to slice the chicken and cook it in a skillet until cooked.

Chicken Fajitas

Chicken fajitas are a quick weeknight meal that allows everyone to customize their meal to their liking. Be sure to serve with all the fixings that your family likes, such as sour cream, grated cheddar cheese, tomatoes, guacamole, etc.

Serves 4; to make a big batch, simply double or triple recipe
Method: Marinate the chicken and cook it fresh on serving day.
Ingredients:

- **1 pound chicken breasts, sliced into 1" pieces**

- 3 cloves garlic, minced

- 2 tab. Olive oil

- 2 limes (or lemons), squeezed for juice

- 1 teas. Chili powder
- ¼ teas. Ground cumin
- ½ teas. Salt
- ½ teas. Pepper
- 2 bell peppers (red, yellow or orange), sliced in strips
- 1 red onion, sliced

To prepare for the freezer: Place chicken in a gallon-sized freezer bag. Add seasonings and mash everything around so the chicken is coated in the mix. In a smaller (quart) freezer bag, add the peppers and onions. If you like, you can either staple these bags together, or place both bags inside another gallon-sized freezer bag. Label "Chicken Fajitas" and the date.

When you're ready to eat: Thaw the chicken overnight in the fridge.

In a large saucepan, add about a tablespoon of olive oil and sauté the peppers and onions until they are tender. Season with salt and pepper to taste. If you like, you can sprinkle a little cumin over the peppers and onions while cooking.

It's easiest to remove the peppers and onions from the pan and tent with foil while you cook the chicken in the same pan. Conversely, you can grill the chicken outdoors or on an indoor grill or you can broil the chicken.

Baked Pasta

(Makes 2 9" x 9" pans to freeze; each serves 4.)
Method: Make casserole and freeze. Bake when it's time to serve.
Ingredients:
- **1 tab. Olive oil**

- 1 small white onion, chopped

- 3 large cloves garlic, minced

- 1 jar (24 oz.) vodka pasta sauce

- 1 pound pasta (penne or ziti works well)

- 1 bag (10 oz.) baby spinach

- 12 ounces flavored chicken or turkey sausage, cut into bite-size pieces

- 5 ounces shredded Italian cheese blend

- ¼ c. parmesan cheese, grated

To prepare for the freezer: In a large pot of boiling water, cook the pasta until al dente. Add spinach at the end of cooking and cook the spinach just until wilted. Drain and return the pasta and spinach to the pot.

Add the vodka sauce, sausage, and most of the cheese blend to the pot with the pasta. Toss well. Season with salt and pepper and divide into 2 9" x 9" foil pans that are coated with cooking spray. Let cool completely. Cover with plastic wrap or foil and freeze. Divide leftover cheese blend and place into freezer bags. Store in freezer with the casserole.

When ready to eat: Do not thaw. Heat oven to 400 degrees. Remove the casserole from the freezer; take off the wrap, if used. Cover with foil. If you used foil in the freezer, just put the casserole right into the oven. Bake for 1 ½ to 2 hours or until hot all the way through. Remove foil, top with the remaining cheese blend and the parmesan and return to the oven for another 20 minutes. (If you need to cook this faster, thaw the casserole in the oven overnight and bake for 45 minutes to an hour.)

www.ingramcontent.com/pod-product-compliance
Lightning Source LLC
Chambersburg PA
CBHW071437070526
44578CB00001B/108